THE BOOK OF CHANGE

How to understand and use the I Ching

Neil Powell

Picture acknowledgments. Titlepage: Mark Gerson – 2–3: Jeff Teasdale/Gulbenkian Museum, Durham – 4: Musee Guimet – 5: Jeff Teasdale/Gulbenkian Museum, Durham – 7: Photoresources/British Museum – 9: Keystone – 11: Radio Times Hulton – 13: Roland Michaud – 14–15: Cooper-Bridgeman Library/Morse Collection, New York – 16: (T) IGDA; (BL) Michael Holford/British Museum; (BR) Jeff Teasdale/Gulbenkian Museum, Durham – 18–19: (L) Jeff Teasdale/Gulbenkian Museum, Durham; (R) Michael Holford – 20–21: Museum of Fine Arts, Boston – 22: G. Mandel – 23: Michael Holford/Victoria & Albert Museum, London – 24: Cooper-Bridgeman Library/British Museum – 25: Cooper-Bridgeman Library/private coll. – 26: IGDA – 27: Snark International/British Museum – 28: Museum of Fine Arts, Boston – 29: IGDA – 31: IGDA – 32: IGDA – 33: IGDA – 34: Photoresources/British Museum – 35: IGDA – 36: IGDA – 37: IGDA – 39: Ostasiatiska Museet, Stockholm – 40: Cooper-Bridgeman Library/British Museum – 41: Snark International/British Museum – 42: FOT Library – 43: IGDA – 44–45: IGDA – 46: Archivio B – 48: FOT Library – 49: Michael Holford/Horniman Museum, London – 50: Archivio B – 52: Bruce Coleman – 55: Maison de l'Asie – 56–57: Cooper-Bridgeman Library/Freer Gallery, Washington – 58: Imperial Palace, Pekin – 59: National Museum, Taiwan – 60: IGDA – 63: Snark International/Musee Guimet – 64: IGDA – 66: Edistudio/Biblioteque Nationale, Paris – 67: Jeff Teasdale/Gulbenkian Museum, Durham – 69: Archivio B – 71: Tang – 73: IGDA – 75: IGDA – 76: Lavaud/Musee Guimet – 77: IGDA – 79: Photoresources/British Museum – 80: IGDA – 84: Michael Holford/Victoria & Albert Museum, London – 85: Michael Holford/Horniman Museum, London – 87: Archivio B/Nelson Gallery, Kansas City – endpapers: Museum of Fine Arts, Boston

First Published 1979 by Orbis Publishing Limited, London
Reprinted 1988 by Macdonald & Co (Publishers) Ltd under the Black Cat imprint

Macdonald & Co (Publishers) Ltd,
3rd Floor, Greater London House,
Hampstead Road, London NW1 7QX

a member of Maxwell Pergamon Publishing Corporation plc

ISBN 0-7481-0204-3

Printed in Italy by G. Canale & C. S.p.A. Turin

Front cover: Early nineteenth century incense burner, with yin-yang symbol of the Great Ultimate and eight trigrams
(Abbot Hall Art Gallery, Kendal)

Back cover: The yin-yang symbol surrounded by the eight trigrams. This arrangement is known as the Sequence of Earlier Heaven, or Primal Arrangement
(Roland Michaud)

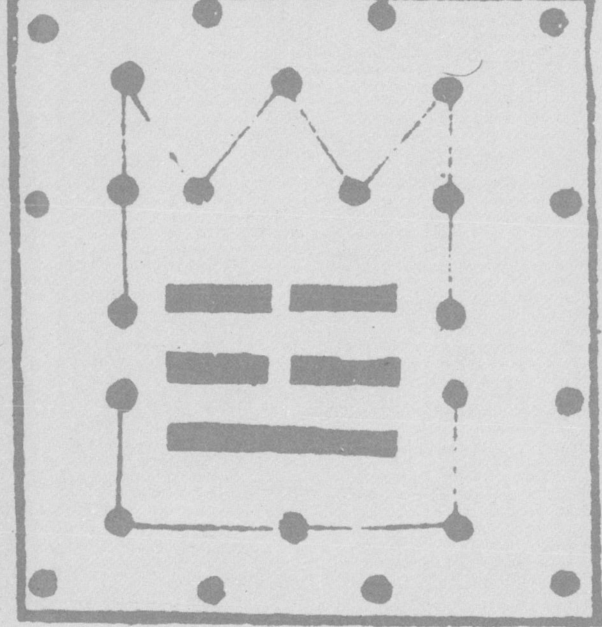

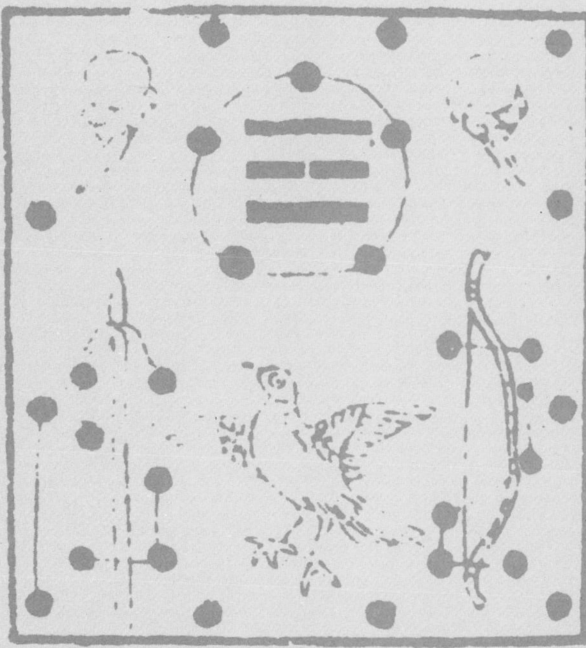

九宮八卦生變圖 血湖地獄變圖

Contents

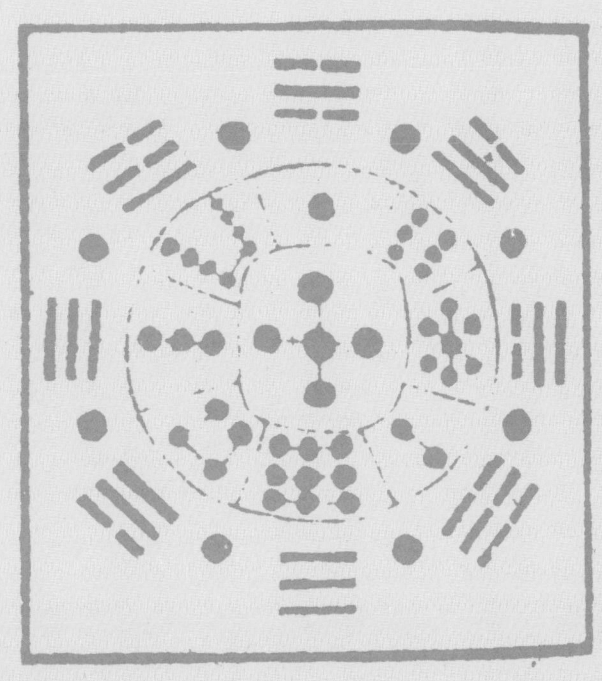

1 Tao: the Chinese way

Three great religions flourished in pre-communist China. The first was Confucianism, an austere doctrine of 'doing the proper thing', an aristocratic philosophy which had great appeal for many intellectuals, particularly the Mandarins who made up the Imperial Civil Service, but had little to offer the ordinary Chinese, were he townsman or peasant.

The second was Buddhism, divided into a large number of diversive and often competing schools, from those concerned with rationalist logical systems to others preaching the severe anti-intellectualism which later gave birth to the Zen Buddhism of Japan – now so popular in the western world. Some of these Buddhist sects had almost totally departed from the simplicity and anti-ritualism of the original Buddhism of India and practised a variety of magical techniques largely concerned with the placation of demons and the achievement of 'good luck'.

Such magical varieties of Buddhism tended to blend with the more popular aspects of Taoism, the faith of the great mass of the Chinese people. But Taoism was much more than a variety of folk magic. It had something for everybody – it provided not only simple charms and ceremonies for the use of the peasant, but a lofty philosophy of 'the Way of Heaven' for those who could understand its scriptures and the many abstruse commentaries upon them, a complex system of magical rites for those drawn towards what westerners usually call 'the occult', and a technique of exercises involving physical sexuality for those who sought spiritual illumination through the channels of the senses.

Confucius, one of the greatest of Chinese philosophers, was nearly 70 years old when, in 481 BC, he said: 'If some years were added to my life, I would give fifty to the study of the I Ching, and might then escape falling into great errors'

The most sacred and basic of the Taoist scriptures was (and is, for the faith still flourishes among the Chinese of South-East Asia) the *Tao-te-Ching*, the Book of the Tao. This work, attributed to Lao-Tse, a sage born in 604 BC, is the shortest of the world's great scriptures. In the original Chinese version only some five thousand characters are employed and, even in the more long-winded languages of the west, translations are usually only some four to ten thousand words in length. Yet, in spite of its brevity, the *Tao-te-Ching* expresses doctrines of such depth and complexity that it has spawned a great mass of commentaries and explanatory treatises; as early as the seventh century AD there were no less than 4,500 of these.

What exactly is the 'Tao' of the book's title? The word is usually translated as 'Way', meaning Way in its religious sense as used by Christ ('I am the Way, the Truth and the Life'), but no English word provides a really satisfactory equivalent, and even in Chinese the word has more than one meaning and different schools of Taoist thinking have used the word in different ways.

The Tao is, says one inscription, 'the ancestor of all doctrines, the mystery beyond mysteries'; it cannot be put into words, only understood on an instinctive level – 'the Tao that can be put into words is not the Everlasting Tao'.

Perhaps the best way that the ordinary westerner can come to some understanding of the inner meaning of the Tao is to immerse himself in the *Tao-te-Ching* and other Taoist scriptures or to examine the practical techniques, from acupuncture to the Chinese martial arts, that are ultimately derived from Taoism.

Neither of these courses of action is easily performed, for the values and ways of thought which find expression in Taoist writings and techniques are alien to those dominant in the science- and technology-based cultures of Europe and North America. Taoist values are opposed to action and material achievement, 'power and learning is adding more and more to oneself, Tao is subtracting day by day'. Passivity is seen as a desirable quality, 'rigour is death, yielding is life'. Law and Order, the twin gods of the policeman and the lawyer, are seen as obstacles to the Tao: 'as laws increase, crimes increase'.

At their most extreme these attitudes make the Taoist into a sort of pacifist anarchist who totally rejects not only all laws and governments as enemies of the Tao but even the simplest mechanical aids to the everyday business of living. Just how far this rejection of material things can go is illustrated by a popular Taoist story:

An intelligent young man observes an elderly peasant irrigating his crops by the tedious process of raising water from a well, one bucket at a time, and taking it to the fields. The young man describes a simple mechanism that would deliver water directly from the well to the crops. 'I know of this apparatus', says the old man, 'but those who use cunning machines soon begin to practise cunning ways. Thus their hearts become cunning, and a cunning heart prevents one from being pure in thought. Those whose thought is impure have troubled spirits, and these cease to be fit vehicles for the Tao'.

With such curious ways of thought as those expressed in this story go equally alien modes of regarding time, space and the material objects that make up the world as the ordinary man knows it.

In the western world we think of time and space as made up of separate things. Thus time is regarded as a flow of separate units – seconds, minutes and hours – each one divided from the others although, in a sense, identical with them. Similarly space is viewed as divided into separate elements, some of them alive, like people and animals, others, such as tables and chairs, inanimate.

To the Taoist adept this displays a vulgar and incomplete understanding of the true nature of reality. For him, or her – for many of the great Taoist sages have been women – everything is part of everything else. Reality is not hard and fixed, it is ceaseless change. The river one stepped into yesterday is not the same river one bathes in today, the universe is a moving pattern, nothing is permanent. All the separations of objects and moments of time which we take for granted in the west are no more than philosophical fictions which are themselves mere elements in the everchanging web of reality. Only by being conscious of his own ever-fluctuating nature, only by abandoning the myth of a unique and unchanging 'self', can man attain the spiritual liberation of being a fit vehicle for the Tao.

This acceptance of the changing nature of reality, this refusal to look upon anything as being altogether alien to humanity, has made Taoism the most tolerant of all the world's religions. In Taoist temples one can find images of Christ beside those of Lao-Tse, terrifying pictures of demons beside those of the tender Goddess of Mercy – all are seen as aspects of the constant flux of existence: all the gods are 'real'. In view of this tolerance it is not surprising that Taoism, alone of the great religions, has flatly refused to condemn 'the black arts' – magical and occult practices – but has instead absorbed them into itself.

This concern with magic has been seen by Christian missionaries and other hostile observers as evidence of the degeneracy of Taoism, an indication that the lofty philosophy of Lao-Tse had become corrupted by 'heathen supersition'. In fact Lao-Tse, who was not the founder of Taoism but only its reviver and expositor, never condemned the performance of ritual magic and there is evidence that occult theories and techniques have been an integral part of the faith since the days of the Yellow Emperor, its mythical founder, who is supposed to have flourished somewhere about 2500 BC.

A Chinese coin, impressed with the eight trigrams that are the basis of the I Ching. The order in which these symbols are arranged is that attributed to King Wen, and is known as the Sequence of Later Heaven, or Inner World Arrangement

Taoist magic exists on many different levels. At its lowest there are the rites employed by peasants to ensure good luck and a rich harvest or to cure sick animals. Such rites are no more, or course, than Chinese equivalents of the charms used for similar purposes by the European 'cunning men' (white witches) and Pennsylvanian hex-doctors of the last century. On a somewhat more intellectual level are the practices associated with such a Taoist school as the 'Pervading Unity Tao'. Such schools teach abstention from alcohol, tobacco and other stimulants, are rigidly vegetarian, worship the gods of all religions, use magic charms in attempts to obtain their desires, and endeavour to communicate with supernatural beings through the use of what is called 'the flying spirit pencil'. This last is no more than a Chinese variant of the planchette used by European spiritualists – a writing instrument is placed within a holder mounted upon small wheels, and each of the group using it places a finger upon the holder, which then moves about writing meaningful messages supposedly transmitted by spirits of one kind or another acting through the motionless bodies of the sitters.

Such activities may appear futile to westerners unattracted to occultism, but it must be admitted that members of such Taoist groups seem to find their practices meaningful and valuable on both a psychological and spiritual level. In addition to this there is no doubt that such cults have sometimes preserved and transmitted Taoist literature which has exerted an influence outside the culture which gave it birth. Thus *The Secret of the Golden Flower,* a treatise which deeply affected the late C. G. Jung and the whole school of western psychology derived from him, was from just such a school.

On the highest level of Taoist magic are the practices of those adepts which, so it is believed, can lead the practitioner to the ultimate attainment desired by Taoists of every level of sophistication – joining the ranks of the *hsien;* the legendary immortals who can fly on dragons, perform miracles such as feeding multitudes on boiled stones and bringing the dead to life, converse with the gods, and produce legions of spirit-soldiers from thin air.

There are many varieties of technique, it is held, which can lead the adept towards immortality and the powers which accompany it. But the best known and most widely practised are concerned with sexual magic, sometimes called sexual alchemy, processes which transform sexuality from a mere channel of physical pleasure into a supernatural rite.

Some of these processes involve the suppression of ordinary physical sexuality, others its almost frenzied expression, but all are based on the idea that the energies of the universe can be classified under two headings, Yin and Yang. The first is passive, watery, pertaining to the moon – female energy. The latter is active, fiery, pertaining to the sun – – the energy of the male. While immortality is essentially a masculine (yang) quality no man can attain it without some element of the yin essences and the converse is true for women.

In full-blooded Taoist sexual magic, therefore, joyous physical intercourse between man and woman plays an essential part, for the visible sexual secretions are regarded as only the gross by-products of the male and female energies which are transmitted from one partner to the other in the course of orgasm and the events leading up to it. The energies of yin and yang are first stimulated by foreplay, then raised to a higher pitch by the use of particular sexual postures – many of them, such as 'the seagull's wing over the cliff edge', given symbolic names – and particular rhythms of penetration, for example a pattern of deep and shallow penile thrusts such as three shallow, five deep, seven shallow, nine deep.

Intercourse carried on in such complex postures and rhythms, it is supposed, greatly stimulates the production of the pure essences of yin and yang. As the act proceeds towards its climax the male adept is enabled to extract yin from the breasts and under the tongue of his partner. Finally comes orgasm; the male and female energies are liberated and exchanged between the lovers, the man absorbing the female energies from the woman's womb through the channel of the penis while, at the same time, he transmits the male energy through the penis and into the womb.

In the past, and possibly still at the present day, some Taoist magicians, both male and female, practised a curious and perhaps selfish variant of this rite. They held that it was desirable totally to conserve one's own energy, be it male or female, but to extract as much as possible from members of the opposite sex. They therefore had intercourse with as many partners as they could, bringing those partners to full orgasm but avoiding it themselves until the desire to achieve a climax was uncontrollable. Preferably the partners employed in this practice were as young as possible, for those who had only just achieved puberty were considered to be paricularly rich in yin and yang, but this was not essential. When orgasm was finally achieved by those who used this technique, it was, of course, explosive – but some adepts deliberately avoided this culmination by methods of physical and psychological desensitization of the sexual organs, although more than one Taoist school regarded this as a dangerous practice.

What purpose is supposedly forwarded by such sexual antics, by the dynamic interchange of yin and yang? Or is there no real purpose behind Taoist sexual magic, is it just an excuse for debauchery? The answer to the latter question is a very definite no. Throughout most of its history Chinese culture has been far more sexually liberated than that of the western world. China, it is true, suffered periods of puritanism and sexual repression, usually imposed by some fanatically Confucian ruler, but on the whole those Chinese who have wanted to indulge in sexual athletics have been able to do so without incurring any penalties (save for being the butt of vulgar jokes), or even any marked disapproval.

Far from being intended as an excuse for immortality the interchange of yin and yang has always had a deeply serious purpose, 'the transmutation of lead into gold'. In other words, the raising of the sexual energy of an individual to a level at which it approximates to the pure and undifferentiated Tao.

This transformation is achieved in 'crucibles'. These are not, for Taoists, the containers used in the chemistry of both west and east, but centres of psycho-spiritual activity which exist in the subtle body – roughly the equivalent of the Christian 'soul' – which underlies the physical body of each and every man and woman. The exact nature of the process used to employ the yin and yang in this spiritual transmutation is too complex to be outlined in a brief article and it suffices to say that the Taoist adept uses meditative, physical and visually imaginative exercises somewhat similar to those employed by the Tantric (sexo-religious) yogis of India.

Almost identical exercises are employed by those Taoists, usually male, who give their adherence to another variety of sexual magic in which there is no partner of the opposite sex. The basis of this practice is the deliberate arousal of the sexual instincts, often by masturbation, but the avoidance of 'earthing' them by orgasm. Instead the physical and emotional energies are sent 'up' from the genitals into the psycho-spiritual crucibles where they are transformed, by similar exercises to those mentioned above, into the spiritual gold of the Tao.

While, as has been described, Taoist magic appears to exist on several levels, it is wise to remember that such a differentiation comes from thinking in a western, not a Taoist, manner. To the genuine Taoist, who refuses to make any real separation between one thing and another, all varieties of magic are essentially one, no more than aspects of the ever-changing pattern of reality. In the last analysis it is impossible to separate the village magician with his charms and hocus-pocus from the practitioner of the most intellectually subtle variety of sexual magic, or even from the lofty Taoist philosopher who does naught but meditate on the lofty words of the *Tao-te-Ching* and its commentaries.

Nothing illustrates this Taoist refusal to divide reality better than the *I Ching*, the Chinese *Book of Change*, an oracle book – that is, a book which provides answers to questions – now widely known in Europe and America, particularly through the medium of the translation, introduced by the eminent psychologist C. G. Jung.

The world has had many oracle books and almost all the world's religious scriptures have been at times employed as such; it used, for example, to be a common Christian practice to open the Bible at random, let one's finger fall upon a text and, should that text prove meaningful, apply it as an answer to the question one wished to ask.

The I Ching differs from all other oracle books, however, in that, instead of regarding the present and the future as fixed and unchanging and giving instructions of the 'do this, do that' variety, it regards both past and present as dynamic, flowing, never the same from one moment to the other. Instead, therefore, of imposing a definite course of action it lists possibilities – if you do so-and-so it will be productive of such-and-such a result.

A similar concern with dynamism and change can be seen in acupuncture, a traditional system of Chinese medicine derived from Taoism. Acupuncture, once derided in the west but now being seriously investigated by medical scientists, differs from orthodox medicine not only in the methods it employs – largely the insertion of gold or silver needles into the skin of the patient – but in the way it views the individual human being.

The orthodox physician regards the sick man as a biological machine quite separate from the rest of the universe. There is some sort of mechanical fault, he feels, and this must be corrected by drugs or surgery. The acupuncturist, on the other hand, sees his patient as an aspect of the one underlying reality, his sickness no more than an artificial separation from the life-giving and abundant energies of the universe. What is needed is to restore the harmony and connection of those energies with the currents of the same energies in the individual. Whether this belief is true or false, whether or not acu-

A Chinese vase of the sixth century AD, with a circular decoration of animals representing the constellations of the zodiac

The founders of the three great Chinese religions: Confucius, Buddha and Lao-tse, seen here seated within the petals of a lotus flower

puncture is effective, it is clear that its underlying philosophy is unquestionably Taoist and, as such, alien to western ways of thought.

At the present day Taoism is nominally tolerated in China. In practice, however, it has been subjected to a severe persecution. Its temples and other holy places have been turned into museums, storage space and granaries, or even pulled down; its adepts and magicians have been forced to perform 'useful work' in the fields and the factories; at times many copies of its scriptures have been destroyed as 'counter-revolutionary'.

And yet, paradoxically enough, many of the practical techniques derived from Taoism are actively encouraged. Thus T'ai Chi, a Taoist system of physical culture, is practised by millions of Chinese, acupuncture is used in some of China's most modern hospitals, and the herbal remedies of Taoist healers are beginning to be scientifically investigated.

In the west there is also a widespread interest in such techniques, but in this case concern with the practical aspects of Taoism is accompanied by a growth of interest in the religious and philosophical ideas that gave birth to them. Today the Taoist scriptures and sexo-magical techniques are studied far more in Europe and North America than they are in China itself.

The I Ching

The I Ching is one of the oldest and most respected oracles in the world. In its present form it can be traced back three thousand years, and even then it was old, being based on more primitive oracles.

It has survived intact through the centuries because wise men in every age have held it in high esteem as a source of profound wisdom and valuable guidance, both in the search for spiritual enlightenment and in the conduct of material affairs.

Its elusive magic has captivated some of the greatest minds the world has known, from that corner-stone of traditional Chinese society, Confucius, down to C. G. Jung. Today it is probably more widely known and more frequently consulted by people in all walks of life than at any previous time.

The I Ching is constructed around 64 six-line figures whose English name is hexagrams. These are made up of all the possible permutations of a broken line and an unbroken line in combinations of six.

All phenomena are the result of the interaction between positive, creative, masculine yang forces, and negative, passive, feminine yin forces. Yang is represented by the unbroken lines and yin by the broken lines which go to make up each hexagram. In this way the 64 hexagrams can be said between them to symbolise all the stages of change and flux operating in the universe, and the texts of the I Ching describe these changes and apply them to the pre-occupations of mankind.

The hexagrams that follow on pages 22 to 87 are each accompanied by several texts. The first text, called *The Judgment*, is the oldest. It was composed by King Wên, founder of the Chou dynasty, after he had been imprisoned by the last Shang Emperor, Chou Hsin.

The second text, the *Commentary*, is one of the later interpretations attributed to Confucius, though he is unlikely to have written it himself.

The third text, *The Image*, is another Confucian commentary. It is intended to explain how the sensible person who follows the I Ching's advice – generally referred to as the 'superior man' – would act at such a time.

The final group of texts, one attributed to each of the six lines of the hexagram, were composed by King Wên's son, the Duke of Chou, who destroyed the Shang dynasty in 1027 BC. These short and often enigmatic lines were written about forty years after King Wên's text.

To each of these groups of texts, the author has appended some explanation.

2
How to consult the I Ching

The I Ching can be consulted in three ways. The first involves the use of a bundle of fifty sticks, the second requires three coins, and the third uses six specially marked wands. Of these three methods the oldest and most venerated is the fifty sticks technique.

You need fifty narrow wooden sticks, each about one foot in length. Traditionally these are dried yarrow stalks, because the yarrow plant grows profusely on wild common land in China where sacrifices were held in the old days. Over the years it assumed a magical significance and at least until the present century was planted on the graves of Confucius and Meng-tse, the two most honoured sages of China.

Due to the popularity of the I Ching in Western countries at the present day, bundles of yarrow stalks can be bought in many bookshops specialising in occult subjects, but if you are unsuccessful in locating these narrow pieces of bamboo or even wooden dowel will serve.

Your copy of the *Book of Change* should be kept, when it is not in use, on a shelf fairly high above the floor, and wrapped in a clean piece of cloth, preferably silk. When you wish to consult it, it should be placed on a clear table and unwrapped, so that the book lies on the silk. The yarrow stalks or bamboo sticks should be kept in a simple closed box on the same shelf.

In ancient China, the seat of wisdom and judgment lay in the north, and those giving audience always faced south. You should therefore place your table in the northern part of the room, and approach it from the south. In front of the Book of Change lay the sticks, and place beside them a small incense burner.

Traditionally, before consulting the I Ching, you should make three kowtows to the floor and then, while still kneeling, pass the fifty sticks three times through the smoke of the incense.

Then compose yourself quietly and think of the question you want to put to the oracle. Try to phrase it in your mind as clearly as possible, and make sure that it is a question which is of real importance to you. Remember that the I Ching does not tell the future, but offers advice on how you should conduct yourself in the present in order to make the best of what the future holds in store.

Next, turn your attention to the sticks. The instructions that follow may seem complicated at first, but work slowly and they will soon seem quite simple.

(1) Take one of the fifty sticks and put it completely aside. It will not be used again but is included in the bundle to make the total up to the magically significant number of fifty.

(2) Using your right hand, divide the heap of sticks into two heaps, separating them by a few inches.

(3) Take one stick from the heap on your right and place it between the ring finger and little finger of your left hand.

(4) Remove sticks four at a time from the heap on your left until there are four or less left. Place these remaining sticks between the left hand middle finger and ring finger.

(5) Remove sticks four at a time from the heap on your right until there are four or less left. Place these remaining sticks between the index finger and middle finger.

You will now find that the sticks held between the fingers of your left hand total either 5 or 9 (1 + 1 + 3, 1 + 3 + 1, 1 + 2 + 2, or 1 + 4 + 4). Put these sticks to one side.

A street fortune-teller in Japan, holding the fifty bamboo sticks. His paraphernalia also includes charts for palmistry and astrology

Gather together all the discarded sticks (totalling 49 less the 5 or 9 you have just laid aside) and work through the process of dividing again, starting with stage (2).

When you have done this you will find a total of either 4 or 8 sticks between the fingers of your left hand (1+1+2, 1+2+1, 1 + 4 + 3, or 1 + 3 + 4). Put these sticks aside.

Gather the discarded sticks together once more, omitting the two small heaps of 5 or 9 sticks and 4 or 8 sticks. Now work through the process of dividing the sticks a third time, starting with stage (2).

At the end of all this you will have, in addition to the discarded sticks, three small heaps. The first will contain 5 or 9 sticks; the second will contain 4 or 8 sticks, and the third will also contain 4 or 8 sticks. Look up the three numbers you have, in the table on the following page.

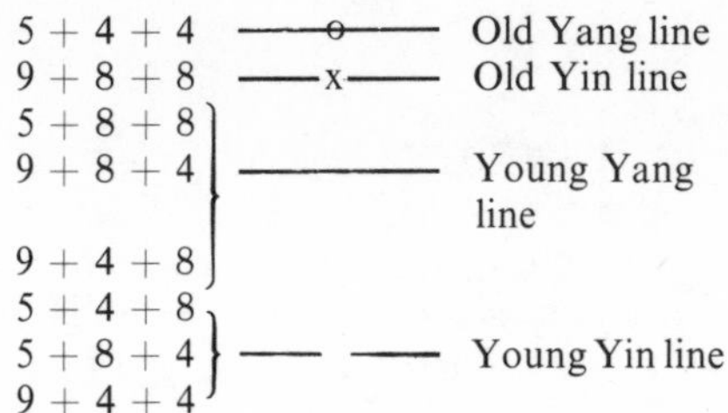

Note down the line that corresponds to your three numbers. This is the bottom line of your hexagram. To arrive at the second line up from the bottom you must gather together your 49 yarrow sticks once more and work through the stages of dividing and counting again.

This must be done a further four times in order to arrive at the six lines of a complete hexagram, reading from bottom to top.

If you look at the above table you will see that there are not just two lines, broken and unbroken, yin and yang, but four lines – young and old yin, and young and old yang.

If your hexagram is made up of just Young Yin (—— ——) and Young Yang (———) lines, turn to the appropriate text and read the *Judgment*, *Commentary*, and *Image*. Ignore the rest, as it is not appropriate.

If your hexagram contains one or more Old Yin (—x—) or Old Yang (—o—) lines, look up the text and read the *Judgment*, *Commentary*, and *Image*, and then read the passage relating to the special Old lines appearing in your hexagram.

Each of the four types of line is given a Chinese 'Ritual Number':

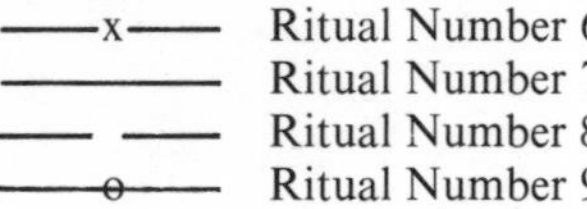

This is why the short passage referring to each of the six lines of a hexagram begins 'In the third line SIX . . . ', or 'In the fifth line NINE . . . . '. Six and Nine are the Ritual Numbers of Old Yin and Old Yang lines.

If one or more of these especially significant lines is found in your hexagram you can take your consultation a stage further. The Old lines are also known as moving lines, because they are thought to be in a state of change and about to become their opposites.

So, an Old Yin line can be changed into a Young Yang line, and an Old Yang line can be changed into a Young Yin line, thus giving you a second hexagram. Read the *Judgment*, *Commentary*, and *Image* of this hexagram and it will throw extra light on your original question.

This ancient method of consulting the I Ching may seem extremely complicated at first glance, but it is a lot easier to do than to read about, and once you have practised a little and learned the few simple rules it will all appear very straightforward.

Whenever possible, the I Ching should be consulted by the method employing yarrow stalks. This is time-consuming and, although the true I Ching enthusiast will always contrive to make time to use it, there are two other methods which are somewhat quicker: these are the methods using three coins (undoubtedly the most convenient of all methods for westerners), and six wands.

The Three Coins Method

The three coins are tossed and, according to the way they fall, the lines of the hexagram can be obtained. As with the yarrow stalks, the first toss gives the bottom line, and so on upward. Chinese coins traditionally have an inscribed face and a blank face, and the inscribed side is given a value of 2 and the blank side a value of 3.

If you cannot obtain Chinese coins, you can use any western coins; but in this case 'heads' is valued at 3, and 'tails' at 2. So a toss of three coins can give you totals of 6, 7, 8 or 9, indicating respectively Old Yin, Young Yang, Young Yin, and Old Yang.

The Six Wands Method

This is the simplest way of consulting the oracle. Unlike the fifty sticks technique described previously, it is not necessary to perform a complicated sequence of operations before you can learn the answer to your question from the oracle.

Here is how you begin. First you need a set of six special wands. These should be about 8 inches (20 cm) long and 1 inch (2·5 cm) wide, and about $\frac{1}{8}$ inch (3 mm) thick. Each wand should be coloured plain black on one side and plain black on the other side with a $1\frac{1}{2}$-inch wide band of white painted across it in the middle.

When a wand falls with the all-black side uppermost this counts as an unbroken yang line (————). When a wand falls with the side showing the white stripe uppermost this counts as a broken yin line (—— ——).

So all you need to do to get a quick answer to your question is shuffle the six wands together behind your back as you concentrate on the question, then roll them smoothly onto a table in front of you as if you were unrolling a small mat.

Arrange them into the form of a hexagram, starting with the wand closest to you, which will represent the bottom line. The second closest will be the second line up, and so on.

When you can see which hexagram you have cast, look it up in the text. The *Judgment*, *Commentary*, and *Image* will give you the answer to your question.

However, there is obviously a limitation to this method of consulting the oracle. By casting the six wands you cannot obtain 'moving lines', so the texts given to the lines of the hexagram cannot be taken into account, and you cannot obtain a further hexagram which might throw extra light on your problem.

The six wands method is a useful way of first approaching the I Ching, but once you are fairly familiar with the oracle you should

A romantic nineteenth century engraving of the yarrow stalks being ritually dedicated before a smoking incense burner

endeavour to learn the fifty sticks technique. This will enable you to make the most of what the Book of Change has to offer.

In old China sets of wands were made from materials such as tortoiseshell inlaid with ivory, or from rare and valuable woods. But you can easily make a set for your own use from strips of ordinary wood of the right size.

Interpreting the Moving Lines

When you have obtained a hexagram without 'moving' lines, only the *Judgment*, the *Commentary* and the *Image* have any meaning for you, but the occurrence of moving lines does not only add significance to the original hexagram but carries you on to a second hexagram.

Here is an example. Assume you divided and counted the yarrow sticks as instructed and came up with this result:

5 + 4 + 8 —— ——
9 + 8 + 4 ————
5 + 4 + 8 —— ——
9 + 4 + 4 —— ——
5 + 8 + 4 —— ——
5 + 4 + 8 —— ——

This gives you Hexagram No 8, *Pi.* You should turn to Hexagram No 8 and read the *Judgment, Commentary,* and *Image*.

But suppose you came up with this result:

5 + 4 + 8 —— ——
9 + 8 + 4 ————
9 + 8 + 8 ——x——
9 + 4 + 4 —— ——
5 + 8 + 4 —— ——
9 + 8 + 8 ——x——

This will still give you Hexagram No. 8, *Pi,* but it includes two 'moving' lines – the bottom line and the fourth line up. Read the *Judgment, Commentary,* and *Image* accompanying Hexagram No 8, then read the texts given to the first line (reading from the bottom up) and the fourth line. These are important.

Now, change the two moving lines into their opposites. In both cases here an Old Yin line will become a Young Yang. You now have a second hexagram, No 17, *Sui:*

—— ——
————
————
—— ——
—— ——
————

Read the *Judgment, Commentary,* and *Image* attached to this hexagram for more advice on your problem.

It may also be worthwhile discovering what happens if the moving lines are changing at different times. If the Old Yin in the bottom line changes into a Young Yang first, you will obtain hexagram No 3, *Chun*. But if the Old Yin in the fourth line changes first, you will obtain hexagram No 45, *Ts'ui.*

The advice given by the I Ching can be expressed as one of four simple injunctions: advance confidently; advance cautiously; stay where you are; retreat. But the texts of no two hexagrams are identical and the advice given in each is both subtle and precise.

You should always bear in mind that the I Ching is the product of a philosophy which was not at all concerned with achieving short-term material advantages, but was rather preoccupied with the problem of acting in a 'correct' way which harmonised with the cosmic rhythms of life. So the advice you receive from the oracle may not take very much account of your hopes for worldly success and comfort – its real concern is your spiritual welfare.

The construction of the hexagrams

To the ancient Chinese, observation of the world around them revealed three factors that were ever-present:

First, the cycle of events – day following night and season following season.

Second, the process of growth and decay – revealed, for example, in the waxing and waning of the moon, and in the life cycles of plants, animals and men.

Third, the polarity of the universe – everything has its opposite, and opposites are complementary to each other.

The positive and negative poles of existence were labelled yang (positive) and yin (negative). Yang included everything in the universe which was masculine, active, creative, hard, bright and strong. Yin included everything which was feminine, passive, destructive, soft, dark and yielding.

Yang and yin were not viewed as permanent and irreconcilable opposites, but as principles that were being constantly attracted to each other, finally to merge but then draw apart again in a ceaseless rhythmic cycle.

One of the ancient Confucian commentaries on the I Ching says: *The sun goes and the moon comes: the moon goes and the sun comes, sun and moon succeed each other, and their radiance is the outcome.*

Cold goes and heat comes; heat goes and cold comes; by this cycle of the cold and heat the year is completed.

That which is past becomes less and less, and that which lies ahead grows more and more; this contraction and expansion influence each other and advantageous progress is made.

The interplay of yang and yin give rise to all the phenomena of the universe, and these phenomena are classified in a 'Table of Elements.' This table is similar to the ancient Aristotelian classification in which everything is composed of various amounts of one of the

Ch'ien	heaven	sky	ice cold	early winter	creative active strong firm light	father	head	horse	purple	metal	northwest
Tui	pool	marsh	mist rain	autumn	joyful pleasurable	youngest daughter concubine	mouth	sheep	blue	flesh	west
Li	fire	lightning	sun	summer	clear beautiful depending clinging	middle daughter	eye	pheasant	yellow	fire	south
Ch'en	thunder		thunder	spring	active moving arousing	eldest son	foot	dragon	orange	grass	east
Sun	wind	wood		early summer	gentle penetrating	eldest daughter	thigh	cock	white	air	southeast
K'an	water	cloud a pit the abyss	moon	winter	labouring enveloping dangerous melancholy	middle son	ear	boar pig	red	wood	north
K'en	mountain		thunder	early spring	stubborn immovable perverse	youngest son	hand fingers	dog	green	stone	northeast
K'un	earth		heat	early autumn	receptive passive weak dark	mother	belly	cow mare	black	soil	southwest

four elements – air, fire, water or earth. In the Chinese system, however, there are five elements – fire, water, earth, metal and wood. These are known as the five *hsing*.

These are assigned rulership of the points of the compass, the seasons of the year, sacred animals, and parts of the human body in particular. Like their counterparts in the west, Chinese sages saw man as a microcosm, a miniature reflection of the universe who contained all its elements within him.

But there was one important difference between the world-view of the Chinese and that of Western man. This was in the Chinese acceptance of humanity as an integral part of the realm of nature, not as a species set apart. The aim of Chinese spiritual disciplines was not the emancipation of man from the world, but rather the breaking down of the barriers that separated him from it. Not union with a supernatural creator who existed apart from his creation, but union with Tao, the all-embracing energy of the cosmos, the underlying ground of yang and yin.

The I Ching was designed to mirror the universe, and could therefore be used to chart the fluctuating fortunes of this miniature universe, man, by reflecting the interacting flow of yang and yin through space and time by use of an ingenious set of symbols.

The positive current of yang is symbolised by the unbroken line ———, and the negative current of yin is symbolised by the broken line —— ——. These two lines combined in pairs are called the greater and lesser yang and the greater and lesser yin to show the basic interactions of the two opposites.

A third line is then added to each digram to represent the three powers operating in the universe: Heaven, Earth, and – between the two – Man. These three-lined figures, or trigrams, symbolise all the basic stages in the processes of change. There are eight of them, showing all the possible combinations of yang and yin lines in groups of three, and they are frequently represented, in Chinese art, as turning in a circle around the interlocking dark and light symbols of yang and yin.

The eight trigrams are viewed as a family, and each is given a name and a number of attributes, as listed in Table 1.

Finally, each of the eight trigrams is paired with itself and all of the others, resulting in a total of sixty-four six-lined figures, the hexagrams. Each hexagram relates to one phase in the cycle of change throughout all levels of the universe and, as every event in the universe in some way affects the whole, the person consulting the I Ching automatically obtains a response which is relevant to his situation.

One of the Confucian commentaries on the I Ching, the Great Commentary, states: *When the superior man is about to take action of a private or a public nature he refers to the oracle, making his enquiry in words. It receives his message, and the answer comes as if it were an echo. Whether the subject be far or near, mysterious or profound, he knows forthwith what its outcome will be.*

The yin-yang symbol surrounded by the eight trigrams. This arrangement is known as the Sequence of Earlier Heaven, or Primal Arrangement

The I Ching teaches that events do not happen arbitrarily, but follow precise rhythms and cycles of change. By deducing which stage in a cycle your particular situation has reached, according to the ancient theory, you can predict which stage is about to follow.

The philosophy of the I Ching

In China, as in the West, correspondences between parts of the human body and parts of the universe were carefully worked out and applied to divination and medicine.

The head was associated with heaven, and the hair with the stars. The eyes corresponded to the sun and the ears to the moon. The breath was linked with the wind and the blood was the equivalent of rain, running through veins and arteries which represented streams and rivers. The bones were thought of as mountains and the orifices of the body as valleys.

Five vital internal organs took their nature from the five elements – the lungs (wood), heart (fire), kidneys (earth), spleen (metal) and liver (water).

By observing the workings of nature, the oracle teaches, it becomes possible to understand the secret rhythms that rule the destiny of man, and learn to use them as a guide in the conduct of life. This is explained in one of the Confucian commentaries on the I Ching, which states:

The sage gazes up and contemplates the phenomena of the heavens, then looks down and examines the patterns of the earth; thereby he learns the causes of darkness and light.

He traces things to their beginning and follows them to their end; therefore he knows the significance of life and death.

A delicate sense of humour is apparent in even the most serious manifestations of Chinese philosophy, and Chinese artists throughout the centuries have delighted in making puns – literal and visual – based on Taoist beliefs and the fundamentals of the I Ching. This painting, entitled 'Passing the summer at the thatched hall of the Inkwell', is by the artist Wu Li; and the painter has made play with his own name, for the trigram associated with summer is Li, the fire. The view is southward to the source of yang, and the artist has used a palette rich in yellow, the colour that is the attribute of summer and of Li itself. And the way in which each part of the picture is closed in on itself by walls or fences recalls the actual form of the trigram

He observes how the union of essence and breath form things, and how the disappearance of the spirit produces their dissolution; therefore he knows the constitution of the lower and higher souls.

Being so closely attuned to nature, the I Ching was used by the Chinese as a useful addition to their lunar calendar. Twelve hexagrams, known as the 'sovereign' hexagrams, were allotted to the twelve months.

The titles given to the component trigrams in the lunar calendar reflect the weather to be expected during each season of the year in North China (Table 2).

The annual cycle was divided into two halves; the first half, which commenced in February prior to the spring equinox, being ruled by the outgoing, positive, masculine forces of yang; and the second half of the year, which commenced in August prior to the autumn equinox, being ruled by the inward-turning, negative, feminine forces of yin.

If, when you consult the I Ching, you find you have obtained one of the twelve sovereign hexagrams, this may serve as a pointer to the time of the year when certain events might be expected to come to pass.

The nature of the I Ching and the superior man's use of the oracle are described thus in the Confucian 'Great Appendix.'

The sages set forth the hexagrams, examined their symbolism, and added explanations. In this way good fortune and bad were made clear.

The strong and the weak lines displace each other, producing changes and transformations in the hexagrams.

Therefore the good and evil fortune mentioned in the texts refer to the rights and wrongs in the affairs of men. The repentance and regret mentioned in the texts refer to men's sorrows and anxiety.

The changes and transformations of the lines symbolise the advance and retreat of the powers of nature. Thus strong and weak lines symbolise day and night. The movements taking place within the six lines of a hexagram reveal the progress of the three powers (i.e. heaven, man and earth).

Therefore the superior man follows the advice of the oracle. He studies the explanations of the lines with greatest pleasure.

The superior man, living quietly, contemplates the symbols and studies their explanations. When starting anything he consults the oracle and studies its advice. In this way he gains the help of heaven, which brings good fortune and advantage in everything he does.

The reverence in which the I Ching was held by Chinese scholars is well summed up in the words of Confucius:

What is it that the I does? It makes known the outcome of things, brings about the accomplishments of men, and gathers within itself all things under heaven. This and nothing more its function. Therefore the sages, by consulting it, would properly direct the aims of

all under heaven, would give stability to their undertakings, and resolve their doubts.

When you have manipulated the yarrow stalks, tossed three coins, or thrown the six wands and arrived at a hexagram, read the whole text through several times, paying particular attention to any moving lines that occur. The moving lines are the essence of the I Ching's message, and though they seem obscure at first, are of real importance.

THE ANCIENT CHINESE CALENDAR

Sovereign Hexagram	*Names of the fortnights*	*Commencing*	*Sovereign Hexagram*	*Names of the fortnights*	*Commencing*
1. **T'AI**	Beginning of Spring The Rains	5 Feb. 20 Feb.	7. **P'I**	Beginning of Autumn End of Heat	8 Aug. 24 Aug.
2. **TA CHUANG**	Awakening of Creatures Spring Equinox	7 March 22 March	8. **KUAN**	White Dews Autumn Equinox	8 Sept. 24 Sept.
3. **KUAI**	Clear and Bright Grain Rain	6 April 21 April	9. **PO**	Cold Dews Descent of Hoar Frost	9 Oct. 24 Oct.
4. **CH'IEN**	Beginning of Summer Lesser Fullness	6 May 22 May	10. **K'UN**	Beginning of Winter Lesser Snow	8 Nov. 23 Nov.
5. **KOU**	Grain in Ear Summer Solstice	7 June 22 June	**FU**	Greater Snow Winter Solstice	7 Dec. 22 Dec.
6. **TUN**	Lesser Heat Greater Heat	8 July 24 July	12. **LIN**	Lesser Cold Greater Cold	6 Jan. 21 Jan.

The art of Tao

All Taoist art is full of symbolism and allusion. In this silk painting (right) the giant peach is the symbol of long life; the stag represents fortune and honours; the bats are for happiness; and the pine-tree, spreading its protection over all, stands for tenacity. In the porcelain dish (below, far right) the shepherdess, a yin symbol, is surrounded by two male and one female sheep. These sheep represent the trigram Tui, the pool of water.
(Below, left) A jade 'Pi' disc, representing the enclosed, yet infinite, nature of the universe.
(Below, right) A jade amulet, with the yin-yang symbol of the Great Ultimate and the twelve Earthly Branches, guarded by a dragon and a phoenix

(Below) Autumn Days, the last of the *Thirty Heaven and Earth Postures:* 'The lord Yang lies on his back, his hand at the back of his head, and lady Yin sits on his stomach but turning her face to his feet. As they have enjoyed twenty-nine positions without pause he contemplates, and, since he cannot see her face, imagines her to be the Great Yin Spirit herself. Her hands have also encouraged this illusion and, as the jade stem stiffens, she raises herself on to it.' (Right) A modern vase, decorated with the magic spirit fungus *ling-chih*. The vase itself symbolises the female sex organ, and eating the fungus was supposed to confer immortality for five hundred years or more. The vase and its decoration thus suggest the way in which sexual intercourse can prolong one's life

'Among green mountains I build a house' (left) is dated the first day of the tenth month 1663. The house faces south, toward the height of yang vitality; behind it, the sharp phallic peaks of summer are yielding place to the rounded yin shapes of winter and darkness, water and the north. Water flows everywhere, symbolising change, wreathing behind the house in clouds of mist that reflect the veins of 'dragon energy' writhing through the rocks. The pine trees and the crane before the house represent the long life to be won by sexual practices and meditation

There are many stories of the *hsien,* Taoist adepts who achieved immortality by diet or alchemy. One of the most familiar is Li T'ieh-kuai (below left) in the form of a lame beggar with an iron crutch. The story goes that once, when his spirit left his body to visit Lao-tse, his own body was burnt by accident, and he was compelled to return to the body of a beggar who had starved to death nearby. On his back he carries a gourd, filled with magic potions capable of reviving the dead

THE BOOK OF CHANGE

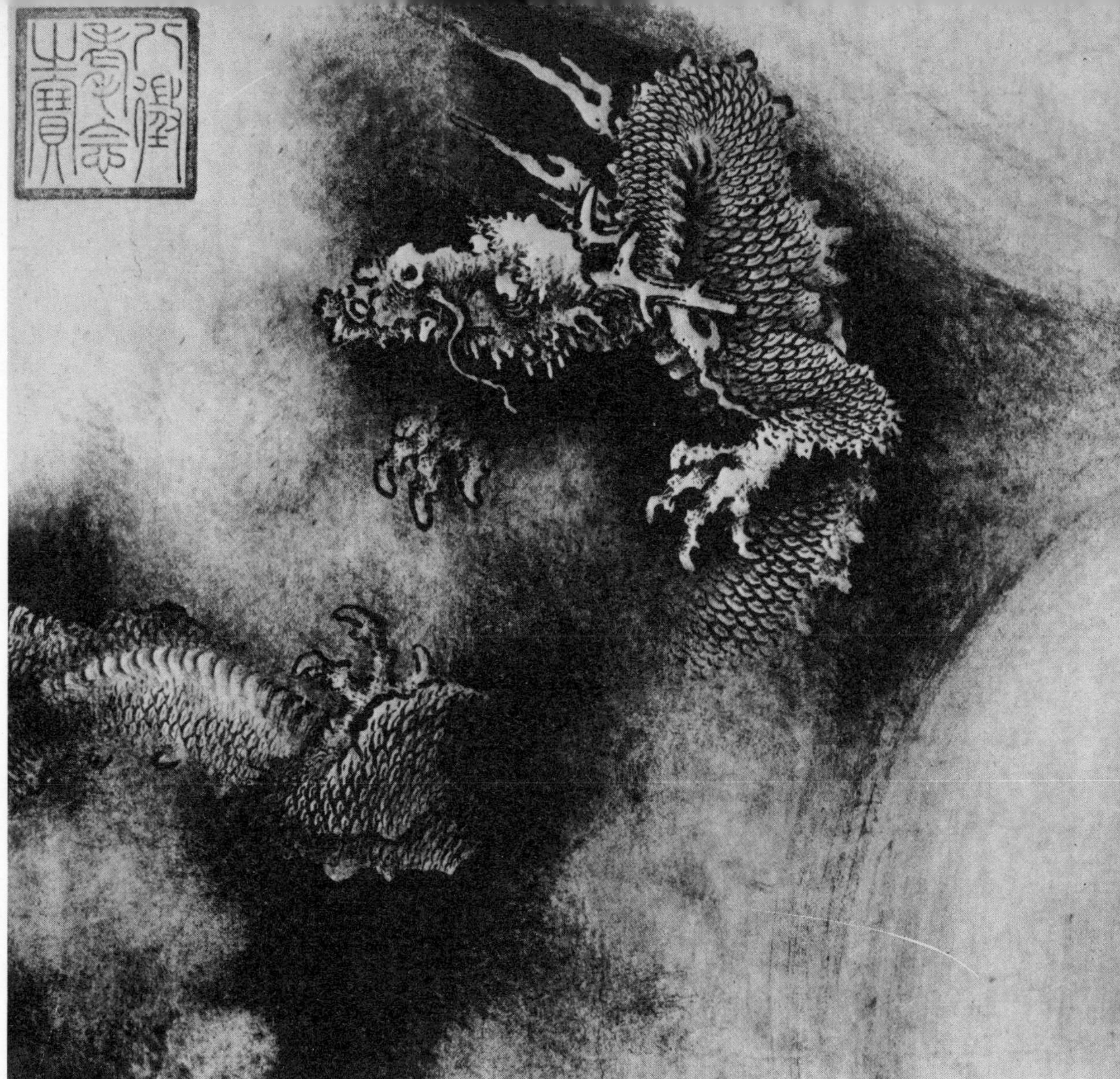

I CH'IEN

乾

䷀

The Creative Principle

The trigrams:

above: Ch'ien Heaven, the creative
below: Ch'ien Heaven, the creative

Ch'ien represents what is great, penetrating, advantageous, correct and firm. It is the originator, the creative. The hexagram consists entirely of yang lines, with the qualities of creativity, virility, activity and strength. There is no weakness or yielding. It is a double image of the trigram named heaven, or origination. It embodies the inner creative power of the lower trigram, representing that of man, and the outer creativity of the upper trigram, that of heaven.

The Judgment

Ch'ien works sublime success. Perserverance brings favourable results to he who is firm and unyielding.

Commentary

Vast is the great originator. All things owe their beginning to it, and it contains all the meanings embodied in its name: the clouds move and the rain falls everywhere; all things appear in their developed form.

The initiated comprehend the relationship between beginning and end, and how each of the six lines reaches its accomplishment at the appointed time. They mount the chariot drawn by these six dragons at the proper hour, and drive across the sky.

Ch'ien transforms everything, developing its true nature as heaven determines, preserving great harmony in union. The initiate appears, high above all things, and everything under heaven enjoys true repose.

The Image

The movement of the heavens reveals transcendent power. The superior man, therefore, nerves himself to untiring activity.

The Lines

In the bottom line, NINE signifies:

The dragon lies concealed in the deep.

Action at such a time would be unwise. In China the dragon is a symbol of the dynamic energy of nature, manifested in the lightning of the storm. The superior man himself is represented as the dragon, and when the dragon flies, the time of action is near; but the wise man, having drawn this line, bides his time for the propitious moment.

In the second line, NINE signifies:

The dragon appears in the field.

It is a favourable time to see the great man. The beneficial forces of nature begin to

manifest themselves. It is time for the superior man to embark upon his chosen field of activity: though he may begin in a subordinate position his innate seriousness of purpose, his sense of responsibility and the influence he exerts will ultimately raise him to a position of power, where all who observe him will benefit by it.

In the third line, NINE signifies:

The superior man is active all day long.
At nightfall his mind is still full of care.
Danger, but no reproach.

The great man increases in his importance; his fame spreads, and crowds flock to him. But he must beware of ambition destroying his integrity. He who can remain aware of what still lies ahead will avoid all pitfalls, and suffer no blame.

In the fourth line, NINE signifies:

The flight across the abyss is not sure
He who is resolute suffers no reproach.

The dragon seems to be leaping up, but is still in the deep. The time of decision has come for the great man: he can go forward and upward, making an important place for himself in the world, or he can retire again into solitude and contemplation. Whichever way he acts, so long as it is true to his nature, there will be no blame attached to what he does.

In the fifth line, NINE signifies:

The dragon flies across the heavens.
It is a favourable time to see the
great man.

All nature is in accord: water flows to what is wet, fire turns to what is dry. Clouds follow the dragon, wind follows the tiger. The great man has made his choice, and everyone follows him with their eyes as he reaches the height of his achievement.

In the sixth line, NINE signifies:

The dragon flies too high.
There will be cause for repentance.

Here is a warning not to aspire too high, allowing arrogance to isolate the great man from the rest of mankind.

'The dragon flies across the heavens' The dragon is a symbol of dynamic energy, manifested in the lightning of the storm. Clouds follow the dragon, as the wind follows the tiger

2 K'UN

坤

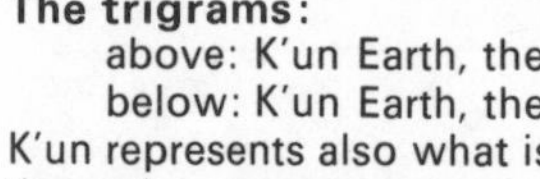

The Passive Principle

The trigrams:

above: K'un Earth, the passive
below: K'un Earth, the passive

K'un represents also what is great, penetrating, advantageous, correct, and having the firmness of the mare. The hexagram consists entirely of yin lines, feminine, yielding and shaded. It is the diametrical opposite of Ch'ien in structure but its complement in character. Male and female, heaven and earth, spirit and matter, the creative and the passive principle, are nothing but two aspects of the same whole.

The Judgment

K'un brings supreme success through steadfast acceptance. When the superior man takes the initiative in action he will go astray; if he follows, he will find his true leader. It is advantageous to find friends in the west and south, and to relinquish friends in the north and east. Quiet perseverance brings good fortune to the superior man.

Commentary

The creativity of K'un is complete: all things owe their birth to it, and it obediently accepts the influences of heaven, supporting and containing all things. The mare is an earthly creature: she moves about the earth without restriction, mild and docile, strong and well-favoured. So should the superior man behave.

(Right) 'A yellow undergarment . . .' A funerary figure of the T'ang period. (Far right) The yellow dragon represents the false inflation of K'un the passive principle

The Image

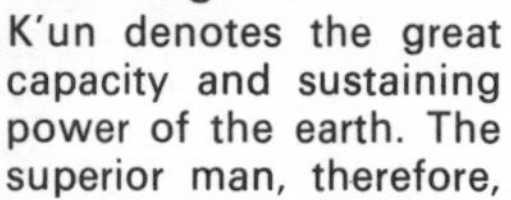

K'un denotes the great capacity and sustaining power of the earth. The superior man, therefore, employs his virtue in supporting all men and all things.

The Lines

In the bottom line, SIX signifies:

He treads only on hoarfrost,
But solid ice is near.

Just as the earth prepares for life in the spring, so it makes ready in the autumn for death. When the first frost appears, the ice of winter is not far away. In life, signs of decay and death make their appearance, but these warnings can be heeded. The wise man, finding that his steps take him on to newly-frozen water, retraces his path and bides his time until the ice is strong enough.

In the second line, SIX signifies:

Straight, square, great; line, plane, solid–
Purposeless, the work still goes forward.

Creation moves in a straight line, generating the first dimension; at right angles it generates the plane, defining the second dimension. Movement in the third dimension generates the cube, the form that the Chinese believed to be the shape of the earth. Allowing himself to be carried forward by the inexorable progress of nature, the superior man proceeds toward his destiny.

In the third line, SIX signifies:

Although the line is hidden, it persists;
Who serves a king should do his work and not seek fame.

The wise man happily leaves fame to others. He does not try to impose his ideas on others, but perseveres at his set tasks, confident that trué virtue will be recognised.

In the fourth line, SIX signifies:

A tightly tied sack.
No praise, but no reproach.

The sack keeps its secrets, but it is also a place of darkness and danger. Great caution is necessary: powerful antagonists should not be challenged, but undeserved praise will later turn to one's disadvantage. The wise man keeps himself to himself, whether in solitude or in the midst of the world's turmoil.

In the fifth line, SIX signifies:

A yellow undergarment:
Supreme good fortune.

Yellow is the colour of the earth and of the middle way: it symbolises sincerity and reliability. As an undergarment it is not shown off ostentatiously, it is the sign of noble reserve. One in a high but subordinate position should be discreet.

In the sixth line, SIX signifies:

Dragons fight in the field.
Their blood is black and yellow.

The black or dark blue dragon signifies heaven; the yellow dragon symbolises the false inflation of the earth principle. When one attempts to fight a way into a position higher than that to which one is entitled, both sides will suffer injury.

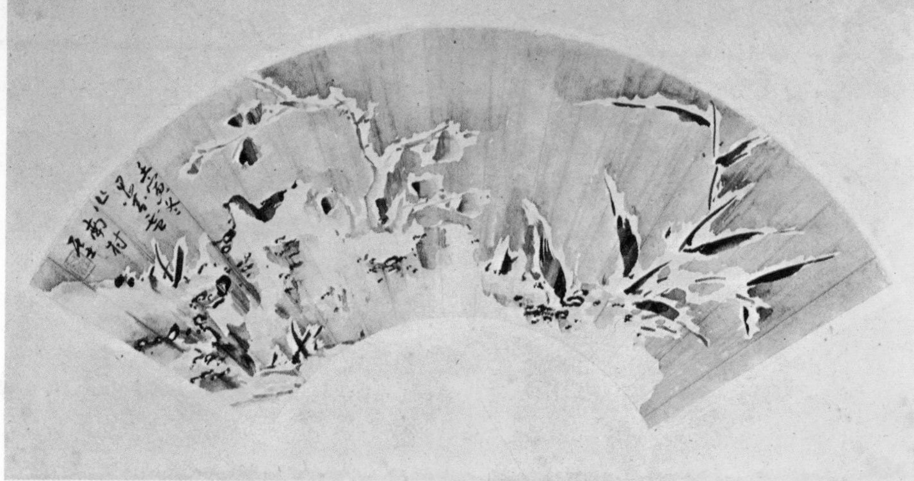

An eighteenth century fan painting of rocks and bamboo in the snow. Chun represents a shoot bursting its way through the soil in the first days of spring

3 CHUN

屯

Initial Difficulties

The trigrams:

above: K'an deep dangerous water
below: Chen thunder and awakening

The sign for Chun represents a new shoot, struggling to burst its way through the soil in the first days of spring. The lower trigram, Chen, represents upward movement, and its image is thunder. The upper trigram, K'an, has a downward movement and its image is rain. There is chaotic confusion: the air is filled with thunder and rain; but the thunderstorm brings release from tension, and everything is calm again.

The Judgment

Initial difficulties are followed by supreme success, the result of acting firmly and correctly. Nothing should be attempted without appointing those who can provide appropriate assistance.

Commentary

In Chun we see the intercourse begin of Ch'ien the strong and K'un the weak, and the difficulties that arise. Motion in the midst of danger leads on to success. By the action of the thunder and rain, all the space between heaven and earth is filled up. But the time is still full of disorder and obscure: nothing can be predicted with confidence. It is advantageous to appoint deputies and helpers, but it is unwise to suppose that the storm is at an end and that rest and peace are at hand.

The Image

Clouds and thunder represent the idea of initial difficulty. The superior man busies himself with creating order out of confusion.

The Lines

In the bottom line, NINE signifies:

Obstacles and hesitation before action.
Perseverance is rewarding.
It is advantageous to appoint assistants.

When obstacles are met with at the beginning of an enterprise, the best course may well be inaction. But this is not the avoidance of action; it is a time to persevere and calculate how best to overcome the obstacle. The wise man chooses those who are to help him in a spirit of humility.

In the second line, SIX signifies:

Difficulties increase.
One of the horses breaks free from her wagon.
But he is not a highwayman,
He is one who wishes her to be his wife.
The chaste maiden rejects his advances,
And waits ten years before she bears children.

As the hindrances multiply, as the horses drag the wagon through the mud of a stormy night – suddenly, here is a mounted man trotting to and fro. But this is not an enemy, it is a friend who comes to offer help; yet his offer must not be accepted, because it will conflict with the freedom of decision. Only after a long time will the right moment present itself.

In the third line, SIX signifies:

He hunts deer in the forest without a guide,
And loses his way.
The superior man, understanding the situation,
Gives up the chase.
To continue brings humiliation.

Obstinately pursuing a goal without seeking advice is bound to result in failure. The wise man, realising the difficulties into which his impulsiveness has led him, retires to reconsider his actions.

In the fourth line, SIX signifies:

The horses break from the wagon.
She seeks the assistance of her suitor.
The time is auspicious
For going forward.

There is a wrong time, and a right time, to accept offered help. It may mean that pride must be swallowed, and that assistance must be sought from one who was prepreviously rejected. There is no shame in accepting help in a difficult and dangerous situation.

In the fifth line, NINE signifies:

Obstacles to generosity.
A little perseverance brings success.
Much perseverance brings misfortune.

The individual is in a position where even his most generous gestures are misinterpreted. But he must not try to force the outcome; it is only through firm and confident actions, carried out unobtrusively, that he will succeed in overcoming the obstacles.

In the sixth line, SIX signifies:

The horses drag the wagon back.
Tears of blood are wept.

The difficulties have been too great: the only way is back to the beginning. But success is not achieved by giving up; the bloody tears will not flow for long, and another way will be found.

Youthful Inexperience

The trigrams:

above: Ken mountain, stillness
below: K'an dangerous deep water

As Chun represents the infant plant struggling to break the surface, so Meng represents its undeveloped appearance. The water bubbling up at the foot of the mountain is the image of inexperienced youth. When the spring firsts bursts out, it has no idea where it is going; but its determined flow eventually fills up the deep, and it goes on its way.

The Judgment

There will be progress and success. I do not seek out the young and inexperienced; he comes to find me. When he first asks my advice, I instruct him. But if he comes a second or a third time, that is troublesome, and I do not advise the troublesome. Firm and correct action brings favourable results.

Commentary

Uncultivated growth. The dangerous pit lies at the foot of the mountain, and to stay on the edge of the abyss is youthful folly. There are perils and obstacles in the way of progress, but the young and inexperienced should be nurtured like a new plant. The intention of the initiate is accomplished.

The Image

As the spring gushes out at the foot of the mountain, so the superior man improves his character by diligent thoroughness in all his actions.

The Lines

In the bottom line, SIX signifies:

The ignorant youth should be
disciplined,
But remove his fetters lest he be
humiliated.

Firmness and severe treatment, even punishment, are of great help in dispelling ignorance and folly. But going on in this way will give cause for regret, for discipline will degenerate into tyranny.

In the second line, NINE signifies:

To suffer fools kindly brings good
fortune.
Understanding of women brings good
fortune.
The son can take charge of the
household.

The young man who begins to develop and to understand the importance of tolerance, as it is shown to him by his elders, will soon himself be able to take on their responsibilities.

In the third line, SIX signifies:

No good will come of a maiden who
loses control
When she sees a man of bronze. Do not
cherish her.

The 'man of bronze' may represent a wealthy suitor, or a figure of heroic appeal. The weak and inexperienced man is compared to a girl throwing herself at such a person; as he struggles to improve himself, he may lose all individuality by trying to imitate a stronger personality.

In the fourth line, SIX signifies:

Bound in the chains of his ignorance,
He suffers humiliation and regret.

The inexperienced youth can so easily entangle himself in fantasies, and only confusion will result, followed by shame. If he persists, no teacher can aid him: he must be left to return to reality by his own efforts, no matter how much humiliation he suffers as a result.

In the fifth line, SIX signifies:

The simplicity of the child
Brings good fortune.

Inexperience is best overcome by seeking the teacher in a spirit of humility, and learning without arrogance.

In the sixth line, NINE signifies:

Punishing the inexperienced youth,
One should not injure him.
The purpose of punishment is to prevent
injury.

As the first line says, 'the ignorant youth should be disciplined'. But the punishment should not be imposed in anger; it should be measured, objective, never an end in itself. It is for the good of the ignorant, not to relieve the conscience of the teacher.

4 MENG

(Below) 'Bound in the chains of his ignorance, he suffers humiliation and regret.' Scene from a fifteenth century silk scroll

5 HSÜ

Patient anticipation

The trigrams:

above: K'an dangerous deep water
below: Ch'ien Heaven, the creative

Water is seen in the heavens in the form of clouds. But clouds, though they give promise of rain, also indicate that we must wait for that promise to be fulfilled. The trigrams, symbolising danger above but strength within, also draw attention to the importance of biding one's time until that time is right.

The Judgment

Waiting. With sincerity, there will follow brilliant success. Perseverance brings good fortune. It is advantageous to cross the great water.

Commentary

The dangerous deep of K'an lies ahead, and though the creative power of Ch'ien drives him forward, he must show patience. Only then will the time come when he can go forward and achieve his goal with success. A journey – but not necessarily across water, indeed it may be a spiritual one – will be rewarding at this time.

The Image

Clouds rise up to heaven, representing patient anticipation. The superior man, accordingly, spends the time in eating and drinking, satisfying himself and remaining cheerful.

'The superior man spends his time . . . satisfying himself and remaining cheerful.' Part of a silk painting attributed to the emperor Hui-tsung, who reigned in the eleventh century

The Lines

In the bottom line, NINE signifies:

He waits at the edge of the meadow
And furthers his plans by remaining still.
No reproach.

Danger is still far off: the prudent man does not take cover, but he does not make himself vulnerable by advancing into the open. He employs the time in preparing himself for future action.

In the second line, NINE signifies:

He waits on the sandy bank of the mountain stream.
There are rumours of scandal,
But, in the end, good fortune.

The sand is soft, and does not afford a good footing. Danger shows itself only in gossip and malicious whispers, and a steadfast calmness in the face of calumny will bring success at last.

In the third line, NINE signifies:

He waits in the mud,
Expecting the arrival of the enemy.

The flood waters are very near, and the ground underfoot is slippery and treacherous. It is not a good place to stand and meet the onrush of danger. With resolution, it would have been possible to clear the stream at a bound, and reach the farther bank, but now the peril must be faced with as much preparation as possible.

In the fourth line, SIX signifies:

He waits standing in blood,
But he will escape from the pit.

Disaster threatens; it is now a matter of life or death. There is no going forward, there is no going back. One stands as in a pit, waiting with fortitude and brave composure for fate to take its course. This is the only way of escaping from the pit.

In the fifth line, NINE signifies:

He waits at the table.
Perseverance brings good fortune.

This is the still eye of the storm, the quiet water at the heart of the rushing rapids. The wise man employs the time in recovering his strength, eating and drinking as he can, in order to meet the struggles to come with strength of body and mind.

In the sixth line, SIX signifies:

He falls into the pit.
Three unexpected guests arrive:
Receive them with respect and all will be well in the end.

All seems lost. All the restraint, all the husbanding of resources and building of strength, seems of no avail. But in the deepest despair, help comes from an unexpected and unsought source. At first it may not be recognised for what it is, but the wise man will welcome it and accept the assistance that rescues him from his predicament.

Conflict

The trigrams:

above: Ch'ien Heaven, the creative
below: K'an dangerous deep water

The upper trigram represents heaven, which tends to move upward; while the lower trigram, representing water, moves ever downward. So the two halves of Chun pull away from one another, producing a situation of tension and incipient conflict. The attribute of the male Ch'ien is strength, that of K'an is subtlety and intrigue; a character combining outward determination with inward cunning will be a quarrelsome one.

The Judgment

Conflict. Confidence is obstructed, and a cautious halt at the halfway stage will bring good fortune. But obstinate determination to go forward against all obstacles can only end in misfortune. It is a favourable time to see the great man, but it is unsafe to cross the great water.

Commentary

No matter what the sincerity of a man's motives, it is impossible to avoid the conflict, but the danger can be mitigated by a cautious approach. The prudent man remains clear-headed and inwardly strong, recognising that his only course lies in meeting his opponent halfway, and that the conflict must not be allowed to become permanent. Advice from the great man strengthens his position, but if he attempts to go forward across the water he will fall into the abyss.

The Image

Heaven and water moving in opposite ways are the image of conflict. The superior man therefore appraises the beginning of any venture with great care.

The Lines

In the bottom line, SIX signifies:

If the conflict is not prosecuted,
There will be some gossip;
But, in the end, good fortune.

The prudent man desists in advancing his views in the face of opposition, and peace is quickly restored. This may give rise to scurrilous talk, but once the conflict has been resolved the enterprise will be carried through eventually to a satisfactory conclusion.

In the second line, NINE signifies:

He cannot continue the conflict,
But yields and returns home.
His fellow townsmen,
Three hundred households,
Suffer no reproach.

The Chinese have always believed that to retreat in the face of superior strength is no disgrace. A man, from a false sense of honour, may try to prosecute the struggle; but in doing so he involves the honour of his kinsmen and may bring disaster upon a whole community. 'He who fights and runs away may live to fight another day'.

In the third line, SIX signifies:

He nourishes himself on the ancient virtues,
And remains firm and constant.
There is danger, but good fortune at last.
Who serves a king should do his work and not seek fame.

He who adheres to the established code of conduct may find himself in danger of losing his position, but success will come in the end. Whatever a man possesses through the strength of his character cannot be taken away from him, but if he is working for a superior he can only avoid conflict by doing his duty and letting undeserved fame and prestige go to others.

In the fourth line, NINE signifies:

He cannot continue the conflict,
But gives way and submits to fate;
Changing his disposition,
He finds peace in perseverance.
Good fortune.

The man, unsatisfied with his situation, attempts to improve it by struggle, since he is now the stronger contender. But his is an unjust cause, and only by accepting his destiny, and adhering to the laws of the universe, does he find peace and success.

In the fifth line, NINE signifies:

To engage in conflict before a just judge
Brings supreme success.

The moment has come for conflict, for the cause is good, and the judgment of an impartial man will bring great good fortune.

In the sixth line, NINE signifies:

Though he gain the leather belt,
Three times before noon it will be taken from him.

The leather belt is the trophy of the victor, the honourable girdle of the great fighter. But although he has won his battle his success does not last: others assail him again and again, and the result is unending conflict.

6 SUNG

Two wrestlers, a bronze from the time of the Chou dynasty, the sixth century BC

7 SHIH

師

A Troop of Soldiers

The trigrams:
above: K'un Earth, the passive
below: K'an dangerous deep water

Water lies beneath the earth, like a subterranean stream about to rise to the surface as a spring. So the soldiers lie hidden when they are not needed, but ready to burst into action whenever it is necessary. The trigrams, combining inner danger with outer devotion, are also symbolic of military organisation.

The Judgment

With firm and correct action, and a leader of age and experience, there will be resultant good fortune without reproach.

Commentary

The name of Shih describes the multitude of the host. The firmness and correctness indicated by the hexagram refer to moral strength. The man who can lead the army aright is fit to be king, for the strong line in the lower trigram holds the whole together and everything responds to his control. Proceeding with a dangerous task is a means to winning the allegiance of the people and the control of the kingdom. The results may distress the whole countryside, but in the face of good fortune how can any error arise?

The Image

Water hidden in the earth is the image of the army. The superior man, accordingly, wins followers by his generosity.

The Lines

In the bottom line, SIX signifies:
The soldiers must set out in good order;
If there is disorder, there will be
misfortune.

Discipline is the essential of all military organisations, and the secret of victory. The troop that goes into battle in disarray is certain to be defeated, and this applies to any venture. The man who begins any undertaking without carefully considering his strategy is doomed to failure; he must not fail to take into account, also, the good faith of those who support him in his various enterprises.

In the second line, NINE signifies:
He stands surrounded by his forces.
There is good fortune, and no reproach.
Three times the king awards battle
honours.

The leader should always be in the midst of his army: he should not be in the van, exposing himself to unnecessary dangers, nor at the rear, where he will lose the loyalty of his men. He who draws this line is assured of success if he follows this principle; he will earn his reward as part of his forces, sharing his honours with his men. Whatever the enterprise. the leader is only ensured of success if he plans to share the profits with his associates.

In the third line, SIX signifies:
The army that carries corpses in its
wagons
Is assured of failure.

This is an image with several interpretations. An army must be able to move quickly and easily, to give way where the enemy force is superior, and to regroup its men where they can be most effective: the army that carries its dead with it is already defeated. It was also the custom in China to carry a young boy in place of the corpse at funerals, who was honoured as his family's representative. Many corpses would therefore each be represented, and none would stand out as the leader. In an army where all are generals, who will fight?

In the fourth line, SIX signifies:
The army retreats
But there is no disgrace.

There is no shame is withdrawing in the face of superior force; even if defeat is certain it is better to preserve the strength one still still posses.

In the fifth line, SIX signifies:
When wild beasts roam the field
There is no disgrace in capturing them.
The eldest son is in command
The youngest carries away the dead:
Persistence brings misfortune.

The enemy occupies the battlefield, looting and triumphing. Now is the time to attack and destroy them. But the fight must not be allowed to degenerate into unthinking slaughter. A strong leader is necessary, who knows when to call a halt to the slaughter before the enemy can mount a counterattack.

In the sixth line, SIX signifies:
The king issues his commands,
Grants estates and titles of nobility;
But power should not be given to the
inferior.

After victory in battle, the leader of the army and his officers are rewarded with honours. But the rank and file should be given only material reward, not land and authority, for their inexperience may mean that they will rule badly.

(Above) Liu Pang, founder of the Han dynasty, with his soldiers, entering a city in triumph. A detail from an eleventh century scroll

Seeking Unity

The trigrams:
above: K'an dangerous deep water
below: K'un Earth, the passive

This is the reverse of the previous hexagram, Shih, where the water lay beneath the earth. Now the water lies upon the earth, flowing toward other water, forming streams that unite into rivers, rivers that flow into the seas. All the lines of this hexagram, except the fifth (the place of the ruler), are feminine and yielding. It is the fifth line that holds them together as they flow.

The Judgment
Unity brings good fortune. Consult the oracle again to discover whether you possess true grace, constancy and perseverance; then there is no reproach. Those who are irresolute will gradually come to him; but delaying too long will lead to misfortune.

Commentary
The hexagram represents inferiors docilely following the lead of the superior man. Indeed, his equals and his superiors will also follow him, for a strong man is needed to hold the people together. Those who first join him will take part in the forming of organisations and the laws that bind them together; latecomers will be unable to share in the good fortune of the community.

The Image
Water upon the earth is the image of holding together. So the kings of old made grants of land to their principal followers, and maintained friendly relations with their princes.

The Lines
In the bottom line, SIX signifies:
True loyalty is without reproach.
When the breast is as full of sincerity as a flowing bowl
Good fortune comes from far away.

The whole is greater than the parts: the content of the earthenware bowl is everything, and the empty bowl symbolises the nothingness of form. The truth in a man's heart speaks louder than his words. The inner strength of the sincere man will attract unexpected good fortune from without.

In the second line, SIX signifies:
The movement to unity comes from within.
Righteous persistence brings good fortune.

When a man understands his true nature, he will join with others not as a servant but as an equal. But if he obsequiously seeks preferment, he is wasting himself. Only the superior man, who acts with dignity and firmness, will find success.

In the third line, SIX signifies:
He joins with those who are unfit.

We must beware of entering into associations with people who surround us, but who are not of our way of thinking; the superior man does not spurn those below or above him, but opens his heart only to those who are his equals.

In the fourth line, SIX signifies:
Join with the leader.
Righteous persistance brings good fortune.

When the leader emerges, the wise man throws in his lot with him. But he must still remain constant and not allow himself to be led astray.

In the fifth line, NINE signifies:
This is the sign of union.
The king hunts with beaters on three sides only,
Losing the game that runs before him.
The people need no threats,
And there is good fortune.

In the royal hunts of ancient China the game was driven only from three sides, so that some had an opportunity to escape. Those who did not were driven towards a fence with a gate behind which the king stood ready to fire his arrows. A well-governed citizenry needs no coercion: they should join in voluntary union, free to express themselves while recognising the authority of their rulers.

In the sixth line, SIX signifies:
There is no leader, no union.
Great misfortune.

No enterprise can succeed without strong leadership. The right moment for unity has passed; now hesitation will only bring regrets when it is too late.

8 PI

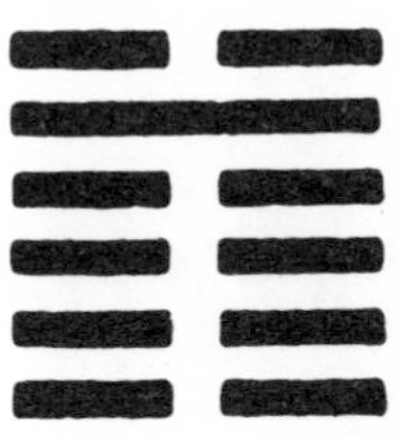

Pi signifies inferiors docilely following the lead of a superior man. The illustration is from a stone-rubbing and represents Confucius with a disciple

9
HSIAO CH'U

The Power of the Weak

The trigrams:

above: Sun wind, gentleness, penetration

below: Ch'ien Heaven, the creative

This hexagram represents the ability, even of the weak, to restrain and impede. The five strong yang lines are held in check by the yin line in the fourth place, the position of the minister. The concept of exercising power by yielding is one that has been developed by the Taoists, who were also only too aware of the weakness inherent in a show of strength.

The Judgment

Success lies in the power of the weak. Dense clouds gather, but there is no rain from the western borders.

This hexagram reflects the situation in China at the time when King Wen, who came from the western marches of the kingdom, was at the court of the ruling tyrant Ti-Hsin: the moment for overthrowing the tyrant had not yet come, and Wen could only keep the more powerful man in check by means of friendly persuasiveness.

Commentary

Hsiao Ch'u combines the symbols of strength and flexibility. The weak line in the fourth position occupies its proper place, and the strong lines above and below it show that there will be progress and success, at the same time conferring freedom upon their subjects. 'Dense clouds but no rain' indicate a strong forward movement, but a movement that has not yet reached its culmination.

The Image

The wind drives across the sky, crowding the clouds together. The superior man, accordingly, reveals his virtuous qualities to all.

The Lines

In the bottom line, NINE signifies:

How could there be reproach
In returning to the true way?
Success lies in this.

The 'true way' is here the Tao: not only the path of correctness, but the way in which one finds this path. The superior man follows the path on which he can advance or retreat as he wishes. It is wise and sensible to avoid obtaining anything by force, and so good fortune must result.

In the second line, NINE signifies:

Persuaded to retrace his steps,
He finds success.

He who can accept that the best course is to retreat in the face of inauspicious events will bring good fortune in the end, but he does not endanger himself unnecessarily.

In the third line, NINE signifies:

The spokes of the wagon wheel are broken,
Husband and wife stand glowering at each other.

In trying to force a way ahead in spite of the obstacles in the way, the man suffered a serious accident: he has ignored the advice of the weaker party, and conditions beyond his control have proved him wrong. But the result is to no-one's advantage, and, quarrelling with his companion, he sacrifices his dignity.

In the fourth line, SIX signifies:

If he shows confidence,
Fear and bloodshed are avoided.
There is no reproach.

Confident that he is pursuing the correct course, the wise man, even though he may appear to give way in the face of opposition, steers a way that avoids catastrophe. Disinterested truth will overcome all obstacles, and the end will be achieved.

In the fifth line, NINE signifies:

Sincerity and loyalty
Make for good neighbours.

In the weaker person loyalty means devotion, in the stronger, sincerity breeds trust. Both result in stronger ties, because either member of a partnership complements the other: the outcome is success for both.

In the sixth line, NINE signifies:

The rains come, and there is rest at last
For he has followed his way.
But persistence puts the women in danger,
For the moon is nearly full,
And if the superior man goes forth
There is misfortune.

The wind, continually driving the clouds together, finally brings the rain. But this success has been achieved by cautious advance, not precipitate action, and it is not wise to pursue matters further. The moon represents the darker powers, and when it reaches fullness it is already on the wane. One must be content with what has already been attained.

Treading wisely

The trigrams:

above: Ch'ien Heaven, the creative
below: Tui a pool of water, joy

Lü means both the proper conduct and, literally, treading upon something. Here the strong, the father principle of Ch'ien, stands upon Tui, which represents the youngest daughter; but, at the same time, the lower trigram Tui stands upon its own firm base and (as it were) treads upward against the weight above. This is a symbol of the love and joy that exist between a father and his favourite daughter.

The Judgment

He treads upon the tail of the tiger, but it does not bite him. Success.

The youngest daughter is the representation of the wild and uncontrollable; the father is the stronger, and attempts to impose his will, and it is his love and correct conduct that will triumph. In more general terms, this means that the stronger, though troubled by the weaker, will acquiesce and do no harm, because the relationship is friendly and without rancour.

Commentary

Weakness treads upon strength. But pleasure and satisfaction respond to strength, so there is no danger. He is raised to a high position, responding to heaven's will, and cannot be harmed or distressed. He shines in glory.

The Image

Heaven above, the pool below: the image of treading. The superior man, consulting both high and low, knows his proper place and gains the approbation of the people.

The Lines

In the bottom line, NINE signifies:
He goes forward in simplicity.
There is no reproach.

Common conventions have little meaning for the man who takes simplicity and truth as his guidelines. He who asks nothing of others may act as he thinks best.

In the second line, NINE signifies:
The man in darkness
Treads a smooth and level path,
And finds good fortune.

The 'man in darkness' is not one in ignorance or who does not know his way, but one who goes forward without attracting attention. He keeps to the middle path of Tao, asking nothing of anyone, and not diverted from his course by attractions of only superficial worth. Alone and self-sufficient, he is content and does not challenge fate; and therefore fortune smiles upon him.

In the third line, SIX signifies:
Even a one-eyed man can see,
A lame man can walk;
He treads on the tail of the tiger
And is bitten. Misfortune.
The champion plays the part of the king.

Though the one-eyed man can see, he cannot see well enough: like a lame man he stumbles on to the tiger's tail, inviting danger which it is beyond his power to combat. So the king's champion, boasting the strength of his lord, may be tempted to think himself a powerful ruler when he is only a man of muscle. No-one should attempt to push ahead beyond the limit of his abilities.

In the fourth line, NINE signifies:
He treads on the tail of the tiger,
But caution and circumspection
Bring good fortune in the end.

In a dangerous enterprise, inner power must be combined with cautious understanding of the situation, and final success will only be achieved by circumspection. Only the man who knows what he is doing and proceeds carefully dare tread upon the tiger's tail with impunity.

In the fifth line, NINE signifies:
He treads with care.
Persistence.
But consciousness of danger.

One must be resolute and firm in conduct, but there is still danger, and obstinate perseverance is perilous unless the danger is well understood.

In the sixth line, NINE signifies:
Watching his step,
And the length of the path that he treads,
Heeding the favourable omens
Brings great good fortune.

The enterprise nears completion. The wise man examines the way he has come, and what lies before him. Only by comprehendding the consequences of all his actions can he know what he can expect.

10 LÜ

履

(Left) 'Watching his step and the length of the path that he treads . . .' A Chinese traveller returning from a pilgrimage to India, and carrying sacred Buddhist scriptures

II T'AI

Peace

The trigrams:
above: K'un Earth, the passive
Ch'ien Heaven, the creative

The feminine creative, which moves downward, is above; the male creative, which moves upward, is below. Thus they combine their influences and produce harmony, so that all things flourish. This is the hexagram that represents the first month of spring.

The Judgment
The small declines, and the great and good is coming. Good fortune and success.

Commentary
Celestial and terrestrial forces are in communion with one another, and all things move freely without restraint. High and low, superiors and inferiors, are combined in social harmony and, sharing the same aims, are in harmony with one another. Yang, representing strength, lies within; yin, representing joyous acceptance, lies without. The superior man is at the centre of things, his fortune steadily increasing, while those of mean nature are at the edges, declining in their influence.

The Image
Heaven and earth unite, forming T'ai, the symbol of peace. In such a way a mighty ruler regulates the separate ways of heaven and earth, marking the seasons and the divisions of space. So he brings assistance to people on every side.

The Lines
In the bottom line, NINE signifies:
When the grass is pulled up
Roots and the sod come with it.
Each in his own way
Finds success in his enterprise.
In favourable times, the man who is called to public service brings like-minded people with him, whose common aim will be the welfare of the people. Going forward according to a well-defined plan will result in accomplishment.

In the second line, NINE signifies:
He deals gently with the uncultured,
Crosses the river without a boat,
Is undismayed by the distance,
And does not favour his companions,
This is the way to tread the middle path.
The superior man can find a use for everything, and is not dismayed by the shortcomings of others, for the great can make use even of the imperfect. Particularly in prosperous times we must not hesitate to undertake dangerous but necessary enterprises; at the same time taking care not to join forces with others for mere personal advantage.

In the third line, NINE signifies:
There is no plain not followed by a hill,
No departure not followed by a return.
He who persists in the face of danger
Is without reproach.
Do not despair at the inevitability of
change;
A setback may be a blessing.
Bad things may be conquered, but they are not destroyed, and may return at any time. We should enjoy our good fortune when we have it, but remain mindful of danger, so that we may persevere against it. As long as a man remains superior to what fate may bring him, fortune will not desert him.

In the fourth line, SIX signifies:
He flutters down,
Not boasting of his riches.
Joins with his neighbours,
Frank and sincere.
In times of peace and prosperity, those in high places mix with the more lowly as equals. This is not pretended for reasons of expediency, but is genuine unaffected spontaneity which is based upon inner conviction.

In the fifth line, SIX signifies:
I am the emperor I
Giving his daughter in marriage.
This brings blessings
And great good fortune.
The emperor's daughter, though of higher rank than her husband, had to defer to him like any other wife. So the emperor's benign action, bestowing his most precious possession upon one of his subjects, brings fortune by its wise and modest combination of high and low.

In the sixth line, SIX signifies:
The city wall tumbles into the moat.
Now is not time for an army.
Give orders to your own people.
Though this is the correct course
Reproach cannot be avoided.
Peace is at an end: the setback signalled in the third line of the hexagram has come to pass. There is no advantage in trying to hold off the evil moment by vain resistance; it is better to try to organise a passive resistance within one's immediate circle. Nevertheless, no matter how correct this behaviour may be, there will still be cause for regret.

'The city wall tumbles into the moat. Now is not the time for an army.' An illustration from The Water Margin, *a picaresque romance about brigands of the thirteenth century. For many centuries the precepts of the* Tao-te-Ching *were followed by secret societies which combined sorcery with banditry, the chiefs of which virtually ruled large areas of China*

Stagnation

The trigrams:
above: Ch'ien Heaven, the creative
below: K'un Earth, the passive

This hexagram is the opposite of the preceding T'ai: heaven is above, moving further and further away, and earth sinks below into the depths. P'i is associated with the seventh month, when the year is already in decline, and the decadence of autumn is everywhere.

The Judgment

Stagnation. Evil doers work against the perseverance of the superior man. The great and good withdraws, and the inferior advances.

Commentary

Heaven and earth are not in proper communion with one another; and so there is lack of understanding between all kinds of men, matters do not have free course, and conditions are unfavourable to the firm and correct behaviour of the superior man. The inner trigram is made up of weak yin lines, and the outer of strong yang lines. So the way of the inferior appears to be increasing, and that of the superior waning.

The Image

Heaven and earth stand divided, the image of stagnation. The wise man withdraws into himself and conceals his true quality. In this way he avoids the calamities that threaten him; but he will not be rewarded or honoured.

The Lines

In the bottom line, SIX signifies:
When the grass is pulled up
Roots and the sod come with it.
Each in his own way
Finds success by perseverance.

This text is almost exactly the same as for the first line of T'ai, the preceding hexagram, but it has a very different meaning. In place of the word 'enterprise' we find 'perseverance', and the implication is not of a man drawing others with him into public service, but of one who persuades others to join him in retirement.

In the second line, SIX signifies:
They suffer and obey;
Thus inferior people find good fortune.
But the superior man uses the time of stagnation
To achieve success.

Those in lower positions would gladly be instructed by the wise man, hoping that he could put an end to their confusion. But he, since he cannot improve matters, does not try: he keeps himself to himself and preserves his spiritual strength.

In the third line, SIX signifies:
He conceals the shame in his breast.

One of inferior standing has seized power, but, realising that he has no dominion over the people from amongst whom he has risen, he feels the first stirrings of shame. He may not admit his doubts in himself to others, but the beginning of self-realisation is the first step to recovery.

In the fourth line, NINE signifies:
He who answers a call from on high
Is without reproach.
Those who follow him will benefit.

The period of stagnation is near its end, and conditions are about to change for the better. The man who leads the people out of the slough of despond must feel the call like the prophets of old.

In the fifth line, NINE signifies:
Stagnation is coming to an end.
There is great fortune for the great man.
What if we fail? what if we fail?
Then bind it to a clump of mulberry shoots.

When a mulberry bush is cut back, strong shoots sprout from the base: so the image of tying something to the shoots symbolises a way of making success certain.

In the sixth line, NINE signifies:
Stagnation is ended.
Stagnation began it, but now there is good fortune.

This standstill in the affairs of men does not come to an end of its own accord. the right man is necessary to lead the people out of the morass and confusion in which they find themselves. This is the difference between a condition of stagnation and a state of peace: constant effort is needed to maintain peace, and if left to itself it will decline into decadence and stagnation again.

12 P'I

否

'The wise man withdraws into himself and conceals his true quality.' A stone figure of a savant, from the time of the Sui

13 T'UNG JEN

同人

Companions

The trigrams:

above: Ch'ien Heaven the creative
below: Li fire, brightness

It is the nature of the fire to burn upward into heaven, symbolising the concept of fellowship or love. The yin line in the second place gives the hexagram its central character, its yielding quality serving to hold together the five yang lines that surround it. This hexagram is the complement of hexagram number 7, Shih, the Troop of Soldiers. Shih has danger within and obedience surrounding it, the image of the unquestioning army; but T'ung Jen is clarity within and strength without, the image of a brotherhood held together by its own firmness.

The Judgment

Fellowship and openness mean success. It is advantageous to cross the great water. Persevering in all things, the superior man advances.

Commentary

T'ung Jen appears in the distant parts of the country, indicating progress and success, 'crossing the great water' symbolising an important journey of any kind. Someone weak comes to a position of power, taking the centre of the stage and responding fully to the creative power. Such a one may well be known as the beloved. The central yang line in the upper trigram represents the superior man, the only one who can comprehend and affect the thinking of all the people.

The Image

Heaven and fire together symbolise companionship. The superior man, accordingly, organises the people and distinguishes things according to their kinds and classes.

Heaven moves upward, just as fire does, but it is very different from fire. As the stars in the sky mark the divisions of time, so human society and all things that belong together must be ordered. Companionship is not just a gathering together of like-minded people: there must be organisation of the diversity.

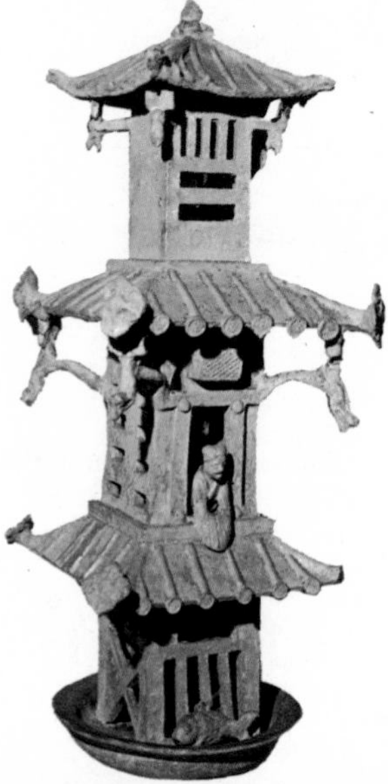

'He climbs upon his battlements . . .' A pottery model of a watchtower, from the time of the Han dynasty, second century AD

The Lines

In the bottom line, NINE signifies:

Companionship begins with those at the gate.
No reproach.

The beginning of union among many very different people should occur in the open, where all can see and be seen, and all are on an equal footing. They start out as friends, with high hopes, and are agreed upon their aims.

In the second line, SIX signifies:

The family bands together.
Humiliation.

Forming factions within the broader brotherhood of man is the first sign of a coming struggle for power. Out of this will come failure and disgrace.

In the third line, NINE signifies:

He hides his weapons in the thicket,
Watching from the top of a high hill.
For three years he does not show himself.

When factions are formed, no man trusts another. Each plans a secret ambush, hiding his true feelings, spying upon the actions of his fellows. For a long time he waits, hoping to catch his opponents by surprise, but there is no joy in this.

In the fourth line, NINE signifies:

He climbs upon his battlements
For he cannot fight.
But good fortune is near.

The first steps are taken toward reconciliation. The wise man still holds aloof in a place of safety, but he does not make the mistake of attacking those whom he thinks of as his opponents, and soon all will be well.

In the fifth line, NINE signifies:

Lovers begin by weeping and lamenting
But in the end they laugh.
The struggles of many bring them together.

Any association will begin with troubles that may cause grief, but when these have been resolved the companions will find happiness. The troubles endured and overcome by others will serve as example, and the help and understanding of their fellow companions will bring them together in due course.

In the sixth line, NINE signifies:

The beloved is in a distant place.
No regrets.

The companions trust one another, even when they are far apart. But the fact that the beloved is in a distant place means that the association is still not fulfilled: the time of true brotherhood of man has not yet arrived. But there is hope and no occasion for self-reproach.

Abundant Possessions

The trigrams:
above: Li fire, brightness
below: Ch'ien Heaven, the creative

Here the flame burns in the highest heaven, revealing all things in its light. The weak yin line is in the place of the ruler, indicating that wealth comes to the man who is modest and benevolent, even though he occupies a high position.

The Judgment

Ta Yu indicates wealth in abudance, and great success.

Commentary

As in the preceding hexagram, T'ung Jen, it is the weak yin line that holds the hexagram together, and it occupies the most important position. The virtues of the hexagram are strength and vigour combined with elegance and brightness. Because it responds to heaven, performing all things at the proper time, it indicates great progress and success.

The Image

Fire in the heavens above is the image of possession in abundance. The superior man, obeying the benevolent will of heaven, supresses evil and advances the virtuous.

The Lines

In the bottom line, NINE signifies:

He has no communion with evil,
Remaining blameless;
Keeping conscious of difficulty
He averts reproach.

The man who is beginning to amass possessions is so far without blame; he has not attracted envy and dislike because he has not yet been forced to compromise with his principles. But wealth can be utterly destructive if a wealthy man is led astray. Only an awareness of the obstacles he has yet to overcome can keep him on the path of righteousness.

In the second line, NINE signifies:

Big wagons are for loading.
He may attempt any enterprise
Without reproach.

There is no fear of failure for lack of resources. The big wagon is ready to be loaded with possessions, and can transport them wherever they may be needed. The man who intends to undertake a great venture must be ready for any eventuality, and must be prepared to entrust his wealth to others who will take a share in the responsibility.

In the third line, NINE signifies:

A prince offers all to the emperor.
But this is not in a small man's power.

The truly magnanimous man should not regard all that he possesses as his exclusive property, but should devote it to the good of the people at large. A petty man attempts to keep everything for himself, to the detriment both of himself and of the common good.

In the fourth line, NINE signifies:

He distinguishes himself from his
neighbours.
No blame.

A rich and powerful man among other rich and powerful men must remain aloof. But provided he does not do this from a false sense of pride, or show envy and attempt to compete with them, he remains without reproach.

In the fifth line, SIX signifies:

He who is sincere and accessible
But maintains his dignity
Will gain great honours.

This indicates a very favourable situation. The hearts of the people are won, not by force and repression, but by benevolence and philanthropy. But when the benevolent man is too readily accessible, he may well be treated with insolence; and insolence can only be kept in check by careful maintenance of dignity at all times.

In the sixth line, NINE signifies:

Giving and receiving
Blessed by the heavens
He enjoys great good fortune.

The relationship between the great and good man and those around him is one of reciprocal benevolence: he gives from his wealth and receives their thanks; they give their love and receive his protection.

14 TA YU

大有

(Above) 'A prince offers all to the emperor'. The emperor T'ai Tsung receiving ambassadors: a painting on silk of the T'ang epoch, from the Imperial Palace in Pekin

15 CH'IEN

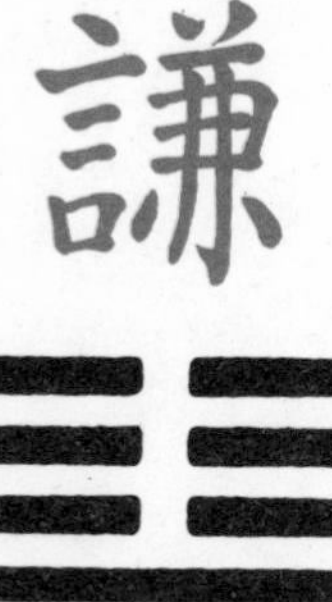

'The superior man is recognised, but maintains his humility.' Figure of a court dignitary from the time of the Han dynasty

Humility

The trigrams:

above: K'un   Earth, the receptive
below: Ken   mountain, stillness

In this hexagram Ken, the mountain, is the youngest son of the creative principle: it dispenses the gifts of heaven, the rain that falls from the clouds around its peak, and shines in the clear air with the light of heaven itself. Ken represents the modesty of great and strong men. K'un, the earth, is exalted, symbolising the way in which simple men are in their turn raised up by true modesty.

The Judgment

Humility engenders success. The superior man, understanding this, enjoys a satisfactory outcome to his undertakings.

Commentary

Ch'ien symbolises progress and success, for it is heaven's way to send down its good influences and shed radiance, and it is earth's way to send its influences upward from below. So it is also heaven's way to reduce the over-full and augment the modest; as it is earth's way to throw down the full and raise up the humble. The demons and gods abominate the over-full and bless the modest, as it is the way of men to hate the full and love the humble. Modesty in a high position shines still more brilliantly; there is nothing higher. As the mountain is hidden by the earth, so the wise man hides his abilities and wealth with proper humility.

The Image

Within the earth, there is a mountain, the image of humility. The superior man reduces that which is too much, and increases that which is too little, setting one in the scale to balance the other.

The Lines

In the bottom line, SIX signifies:

The superior man
Is even modest about his modesty.
He may cross the great water
And find good fortune.

Any major undertaking is increased in difficulty when the participants insist upon their individual contributions being suitably recognised; but those who approach a problem without pride or concern for their personal standing will solve it quickly and simply.

In the second line, SIX signifies:

Modesty itself achieves recognition.
Persistence brings good fortune.

He who is seen to be truly modest will be honoured for it, and success will be his if he adheres to his path.

In the third line, NINE signifies:

The superior man is recognised
But maintains his humility.
He brings all matters to conclusion.
Good fortune.

Success now begins to be apparent, but the wise man is not dazzled by fame: he remains humble, endearing himself to the people about him and working steadily to win their loyalty and support for his future enterprises.

In the fourth line, SIX signifies:

Proper humility
And nothing that is not proper humility
In all his actions.

This is the line representing the minister, the intermediary who transmits the orders of the ruler above, and represents the desires of the people below. True modesty is the sign of confidence in one's position; it should not be permitted to degenerate into servility.

In the fifth line, SIX signifies:

Employ your neighbours
Without boasting of your riches.
Attack with vigour
All is propitious.

He who occupies a position of responsibility, modest though he be, must engage the help of others at times to carry out his plans.

In the sixth line, SIX signifies:

Modesty achieves recognition.
He sets his army on the march
But only to punish his own city and land.

It is often the hardest thing of all for a truly modest man to recognise the moment at which he should impose his will upon those around him. But, provided the discipline is just and necessary, he will be honoured for his actions.

Anticipation

The trigrams:

above: Chen thunder and awakening
below: K'un Earth, the receptive

The attributes of the upper trigram, Chen, are movement and danger; the attributes of the lower, K'un, are passivity and obedience. The movement, meeting devotion, inspires enthusiasm. The strong yang line in the fourth place, the place of the minister, demands obedience from all the weak yin lines; but there is an inherent danger in this arrangement.

The Judgment

It is advantageous to establish a number of tributary princes, and place the army in a state of readiness.

Commentary

The thunder awakes in heaven, and the earth is docile below. The sun and the moon keep their courses, and the four seasons do not change their appointed times. So action according to the will of heaven gives rise to anticipation and calm confidence. The sage also follows heaven's will, and the people follow his judgment with little need for punishment or for any form of penalty. Great indeed are the moment and the meaning of Yü!

The Image

Thunder bursts from the earth into heaven. In such a way did the ancient kings do honour to heaven and its supreme lord with solemn music and appropriate sacrifice, remembering also in this way their revered ancestors.

The Lines

In the bottom line, SIX signifies:

He proclaims his anticipation of pleasure
An evil omen.

Here the lowly person looks forward selfishly to his own satisfaction; he boasts arrogantly of what he desires the near future to bring him, and so invites his own misfortune.

In the second line, SIX signifies:

He is firm as a rock
But not the whole day.
Persistence brings success.

The wise man is not led away by illusion: he sees what is to come without dissipating his energies in unnecessary actions, and knows exactly the right moment at which to move. Adherence to this way will bring him good fortune.

In the third line, SIX signifies:

Ignorant anticipation brings regrets.
Hesitation leads to repentance.

The inferior man looks upward, placing his reliance upon those above him without understanding that he too should take action. If he does not appreciate the right moment for movement he will regret it.

In the fourth line, NINE signifies:

He is the source
Of harmony and satisfaction,
And achieves great things.
Have no doubts.
Gather friends around you
As the clasp gathers the hair.

The superior man is an inspiration to all, and inspires joyful anticipation through his own confidence and freedom from hesitation. He gathers and holds men together by the support he affords them.

In the fifth line, SIX signifies:

He is constantly sick
But does not die.

Continuing to look forward, he finds himself obstructed at every turn. But provided he does not expend his hopeful anticipation in empty enthusiasm he will survive.

In the sixth line, SIX signifies:

His anticipation is deluded,
Devoted to self-satisfaction;
But if he changes his course,
Even when all seems completed,
There is no blame.

It is easy to be led astray by foolish enthusiasm, but even at the last moment a sober awakening can save the situation.

16 YÜ

豫

'It is advantageous to . . . place the army in a state of readiness.' A terracotta relief from the Han dynasty

17 SUI

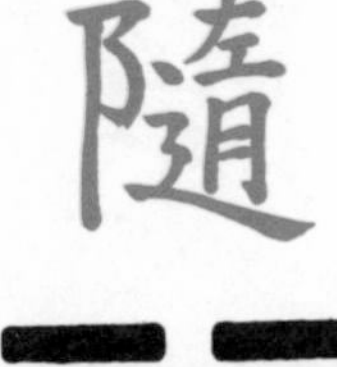

Allegiance

The trigrams:

above: Tui a pool of water, joy
below: Chen thunder and awakening

Above is joy, the youngest daughter; below is awakening, the eldest son. So the awakening interest of the older man is excited by the joyous movement of the young girl; he defers to her and shows her consideration, but in due course she will follow him.

The Judgment

Compliance in the beginning leads to ultimate success. Firmness and rectitude are advantageous, and there is no blame.

Commentary

In Sui the strong trigram places itself below the weak; in the two we see the combination of movement and pleasure. The whole universe complies with what the hour dictates: a leader must adjust his actions to the situation; a follower must adjust his actions to those of his leader. But just as the leader should not ask others to follow him unless his path is the right one, so his followers must assure themselves of his rectitude.

The Image

Thunder rumbles below the surface of the pool. As darkness falls, the superior man goes into his house to rest.

The Lines

In the bottom line, NINE signifies:

He changes the object of his pursuit.
Persistence brings good fortune.
Going forth from his door
And meeting with those outside
He attains achievement.

The wise man will not maintain his allegiance to a belief that is no longer supportable: when the time is right, confidence in his judgment will lead on to success. He must be prepared to listen to the opinions of others, and so form his own, deciding whether he will throw in his lot with a leader, or whether he himself will lead.

In the second line, SIX signifies:

He who clings to the little boy
Loses the strong man.

The 'little boy' represents the first allegiance, which may have been to principles that were not properly thought out, or which were applicable to a situation that no longer exists. It is a time to make more mature decisions, and transfer allegiance to a new leader or moral system.

In the third line, SIX signifies:

He who clings to the strong man
Loses the little boy,
But gains what he desires.
Persistence is advantageous.

In giving up an old allegiance, one naturally loses something: the joy of first experiencing a belief in a cause, the excitement of a first love that can never be recaptured. With maturity, one gives up the unmixed happiness of youth, the pleasure of the absence of responsibility. But the wise man is satisfied within himself as his personality develops and he begins to understand what he wants.

In the fourth line, NINE signifies:

Allegiance brings success,
But persisting in the same course
Brings misfortune
Taking his own way with sincerity
How can he be blamed?

There are dangers in blind allegiance, both for the followers and for the followed. Those who follow are often not honest in their intentions, seeking personal advancement and maintaining their positions by flattery and subservience; and their leader, becoming accustomed to their insincere attentions, will suffer misfortune and eventually lose both his followers and his own position. His only hope is to pursue his own course sincerely and with conviction.

In the fifth line, NINE signifies:

Trusting in goodness.
Good fortune.

This line reiterates the significance of the line before. He who knows in his heart what is right must follow it without deviation.

In the sixth line, SIX signifies:

Sincere, he secures allegiance
And is himself more firmly bound.
The emperor makes sacrifices
Upon the Western Mountain.

In the days of the Chou dynasty, the rulers honoured great sages by affording them, at their death, a place in the royal family's temple of ancestors. The first part of the interpretation is usually taken to mean that the sage, although he himself has reached the furthest stages of his development, is constrained by the demands of his followers; it can also mean that one who becomes the unchallenged leader will still be bound to his followers by the responsibility he has assumed.

The superior man, addressing himself to the people, rouses them up and strengthens his resolve.

18 KU

Arresting Decay

The trigrams:

above: Ken mountain, stillness
below: Sun wind, gentleness

The Chinese character *ku* is said to represent 'a bowl in whose contents worms are breeding'. This is because the gentleness and indifference of the lower trigram Sun has been covered by the unmoving solidity of the upper trigram Ken; in these enclosed conditions the expected result is stagnation, fermentation and decay. But just as natural decay can be controlled to provide desirable fermentation products, such as soy sauce or rice wine; so the condition of decay represented by Ku can be arrested and exploited.

The Judgment

Proper control of decay affords progress and success. It is advantageous to cross the great water. Three days before the beginning; three days after.

As has already been pointed out, 'crossing the great water' symbolises any important undertaking, whether it involves a journey or not. The passage 'three days before the beginning; three days after' has provoked much discussion among commentators. In any properly controlled fermentation, there is an initial period before the process really begins to 'work', and another period at the end of which it is important to arrest fermentation before unwelcome decomposition products are formed. The inception and growth of some new idea may therefore be likened in many details to the process of fermentation.

Commentary

In Ku we have the strong and immovable above, the weak and pliant below. But control of the processes of decay leads to good order everywhere under heaven, so that he who goes firmly forward will come to business that must be dealt with. The ending of confusion marks the beginning of order.

The Image

The wind blows at the foot of the mountain. The superior man, addressing himself to the people, rouses them up and strengthens his resolve.

The Lines

In the bottom line, SIX signifies:

A son repairs the errors of his father.
A good son, redeeming the reputation of his father.
At first, danger
But in the end, good fortune.

The father is the representative of convention and tradition, perhaps the ruler of a state, who has allowed the vitality of himself and his country to degenerate into mere form and custom. The son symbolises the vigour of youth, a new leader who is able to revitalise the state: but before he emerges, there is great danger that the existing system will destroy itself.

In the second line, NINE signifies:

A son repairs the errors of his mother.
But he should not be too inflexible.

Here the errors have not been committed by a strong man, but out of weakness. In setting things right, a degree of kindness and consideration is necessary.

In the third line, NINE signifies:

A son repairs the errors of his father.
There will be some remorse
But no great blame.

Here the young man has been too precipitate in arresting the processes of decay, like one who stops the fermentation of a wine prematurely. But too much energy is better than too little, and so, although his hasty actions may cause him certain regrets, he is free of reproach.

In the fourth line, SIX signifies:

The son condones the errors of his father.
Persisting, he falls into disgrace.

The significance of Ku lies in recognising the processes of decay, and in understanding the right moment at which to bring them to a stop. The indulgent son who is not confident enough to put right the mistakes of the past will bring humiliation upon himself as well as on his father.

In the fifth line, SIX signifies:

The son repairs the errors of his father
And wins praise.

The fifth line is the position of the ruler: the true leader receives acclaim for his actions in arresting the process of decay, particularly in that he also accepts responsibility for the previous shortcomings of others.

In the sixth line, NINE signifies:

He does not serve the emperor
But seeks higher goals.

There are some who do not feel themselves obliged to concern themselves with worldly affairs, but who prefer to withdraw into their private thoughts. This withdrawal is justified when the superior man turns his mind to spiritual matters; for the purpose of the sage is not to redeem the present but to create the values of the future.

(Above, left) 'He does not serve the emperor but seeks higher goals.' An immortal in meditation; a watercolour of the Yüan epoch

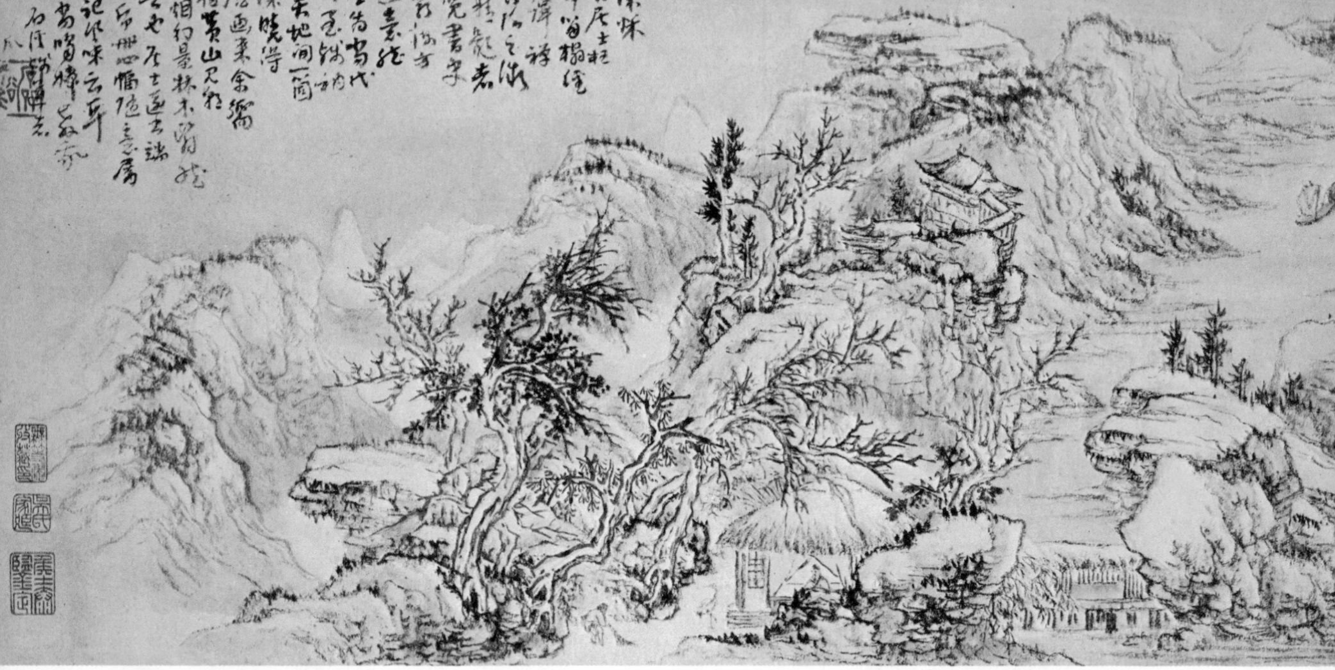

19 LIN

臨

Approaching

The trigrams:

above: K'un Earth, the passive
below: Tui a pool of water, joy

This hexagram is associated with the twelfth month of the year, from January to February, when the days gradually begin to lengthen once again, and the word *lin* has a number of different meanings that are only roughly encompassed by the word 'approaching'. Fundamentally it may be translated as 'becoming great', with an extension of meaning to include the idea of something strong and superior approaching something of lower standing, and from this to the idea of a man in high position condescending toward those below him.

The Judgment

Lin indicates great progress and success; persistence will be advantageous. But in the eight month there will be misfortune.

Commentary

In Lin we see the strong yang lines moving upward into the compliance of the upper yin lines. It is a time of joy and hopeful progress as spring approaches; determination and perseverance help us to attain success. But spring and summer are succeeded by autumn, the time of decay, and the next hexagram shows the reversal of this one.

The Image

The earth above the lake is the image of approaching. The superior man, accordingly, is inexhaustible in his desire to teach, and his tolerance and care for the people are unlimited.

The Lines

In the bottom line, NINE signifies:

They approach together.
Persistence means good fortune.

The reference here is to the first and second yang lines, which are both moving upward. Good influences begin to exert themselves, and likeminded men of goodwill cooperate. Nevertheless, although it is wise to follow the general trend, only adherence to what is right will bring final success.

In the second line, NINE signifies:

They approach together.
Good fortune:
Everything is favourable.

The situation is still full of promise: everybody is cooperating, and all matters are going forward. But this is on a material level: although success shines on everything there is no true spiritual basis to people's actions.

In the third line, SIX signifies:

He approaches in comfort
But gains no advantage.
If there is remorse
There is no reproach.

When a man achieves power and influence he may become over confident, slacken his efforts, and lose all the advances he has made. But if he recognises his errors in time, he will be free from blame.

In the fourth line, SIX signifies:

They come together.
There is no reproach.

While the three lower lines represent a man rising to power and influence, the three upper lines of the hexagram represent the attitude of persons of higher rank to those below them. Here a rich and successful man draws a man of acknowledged ability into his own circle.

In the fifth line, SIX signifies:

Wisdom approaches.
This is the way of the great prince.
Good fortune.

The great ruler must have about him men of ability; his personal wisdom lies in how he selects the right people to advise him. And in allowing those he has chosen to exercise their powers of decision, he appropriately attains success.

In the sixth line, SIX signifies:

Magnanimity approaches.
Good fortune. No reproach.

The great initiate returns to the world, for his desire to teach, and his care for his disciples, are without limit. This means great good fortune for all the men whom he gathers about him; and for himself, there is no blame.

(Above) Winter landscape, a painting by Ts'an dated 1666. All the shapes of the landscape and the trees are rounded in yin forms. Apart from the earth above the lake, 'the image of Lin', the only other predominant material is wood, the 'element' associated with winter

Contemplation

The trigrams:

above: Sun wind, gentleness, penetration
below: K'un Earth, the passive

The word *kuan* possesses two related but opposed meanings in Chinese; by a slight change in tonal stress it can be made to mean both contemplating and being contemplated. The dual implications can perhaps be better understood if the hexagram is seen as a representation of one of those scenic gateways that were formerly erected on high hills in China. Such an erection formed a landmark that could be seen for miles around, but it also afforded a vantage point commanding a wide view of the countryside. In the same way, someone who raises himself to a position in which he is able to contemplate the rest of humanity at the same time puts himself up for inspection by the crowd.

The Judgment

Kuan represents the worshipper who has washed his hands, but not yet made the offering. Impressed by his sincerity, all look up to him.

Commentary

Kuan combines the trigrams representing docility and flexibility; the hexagram is ruled from on high by the yang lines in fifth and sixth place, and the weak yin lines look up from below. When we contemplate the transcendental ways of heaven, we observe how the four seasons follow one another without deviation. The sages, pursuing the same way, have given their instructions, and all under heaven submit to them.

The Image

The wind moves over the earth. So did the kings of old visit all parts of the kingdom, to see their people and give them instruction.

The Lines

In the bottom line, SIX signifies:
Contemplation like a child
Brings no reproach to the inferior man;
But for the superior man, humiliation.

The child watches from a distance, innocently but without understanding. There is a wise man at hand, not understood by the ordinary people; they do not suffer from their lack of understanding because he brings them benefits. But for the superior man such lack of comprehension is shameful.

In the second line, SIX signifies:
Contemplation through the crack of the door
Is sufficient only for a housewife.

Watching through the door-crack, looking outward from within, one sees a great deal but it is always the same view: it is related always to one's personal domestic needs. A man (or a woman) who intends to take part in public life must have a much broader outlook than this.

In the third line, SIX signifies:
Contemplation of ourselves
Determines the choice
Between advance and retreat.

The third line is the point of transition. It is no longer sufficient to observe the world with the innocent eye of the child, or from a self-centred viewpoint. One must strive to acquire objectivity by looking inward and observing one's feelings and emotions, and learning from these, one begins to plan the future development of one's life.

In the fourth line, SIX signifies:
Contemplating the condition of the kingdom,
He decides to seek a place at court
And flourishes.

A man who understands the ways in which a kingdom is ruled should be given a position of authority; but he will be there more as a guest, acting on his own initiative, than as a minister of the king.

In the fifth line, NINE signifies:
Contemplating his life,
The superior man is without reproach.

The man in a position of authority over others should be ready at all times to examine his motives and his past record. But he will not be brooding over past mistakes: he will be examining his influence upon others and, if this influence is good, he will enjoy the satisfaction of a career without blame.

In the sixth line, NINE signifies:
Contemplating himself,
The superior man is without reproach.

This is the highest type of man who, after the deepest self-examination, has finally excluded all selfish interests. Liberated from his ego, he can contemplate the transcendental ways of heaven.

20 KUAN

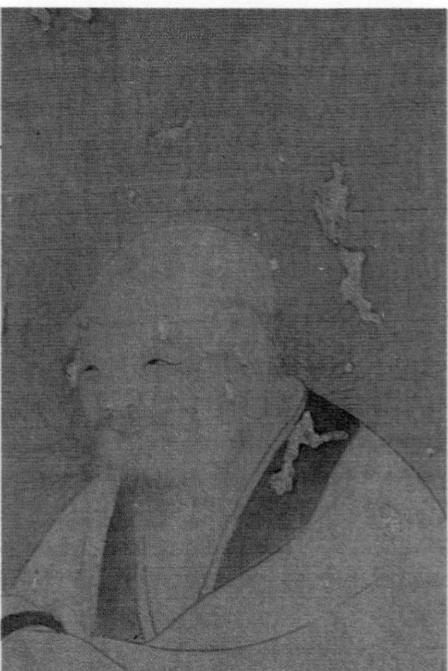

Lao-tse, the author of the Tao-te-Ching, *and founder of the Taoist religion*

21 SHIH HO

噬嗑

Biting Through

The trigrams:
above: Li fire, brightness
below: Chen thunder and awakening

This hexagram is thought of as representing a mouth; the yang line in fourth place is something through which the teeth are biting. When this something has been bitten through, the mouth will be closed, obstacles cleared away and problems resolved.

The Judgment

Shih Ho signifies successful progress. It is advantageous to seek justice.

Commentary

Union is brought about by biting through the intervening obstacles, and the hexagram indicates successful progress. Yang and yin lines are equally divided in the figure: thunder and movement are denoted by the lower trigram, brightness and intelligence by the upper. Thunder and lightning are the manifestation of the sudden release of built-up tension in nature. A yin line occupies the fifth place, the place of the ruler; although this is not its proper position, it is advantageous for the processes of law.

The Image

Thunder and lightning are the symbol of biting through. The kings of old, therefore, framed their laws with care, making the punishment fit the crime.

The Lines

In the bottom line, NINE signifies:
His feet are locked in the stocks
His toes are gone.
No reproach.

The intrepretation of this line has provoked much disagreement among Chinese scholars. The first and sixth lines are considered to represent the man who suffers punishment, the rest represent those who impose the penalties. For western readers the stocks is only a mild form of punishment, and they have interpreted 'his toes are gone' as meaning the toes are hidden by the wooden beam of the stocks; on the other hand, cutting off a man's toes was a specific Chinese punishment, and the penalty described here may be a rather more severe one than is generally supposed. But no matter whether the punishment is light or severe, this line indicates plainly that it is fully justified.

In the second line, SIX signifies:
Biting through tender meat
His nose is gone.
No reproach.

Again this line is open to different interpretations. Some commentators translate it as meaning that the subject is so concerned to see justice done that he 'cuts off his nose to spite his own face'. Others merely see the nose hidden by the depth of the meat into which he has bitten, meaning that he loses sight of clemency in his pursuit of the wrong-doer. Again, however, it is worth remembering that cutting off a felon's nose is a specific punishment, and the verse makes it clear that, although this may be too severe a penalty, it is nevertheless without blame.

In the third line, SIX signifies:
Biting through dried meat
He injures himself.
There is some humiliation
But no reproach.

Here the punishment is being carried out by someone without sufficient power and authority, and in performing it he does harm to himself. However, since the punishment was necessary, and he was performing his duty, he will soon recover and will not be blamed.

In the fourth line, NINE signifies:
Biting through dried gristle and bone
He receives the arrows demanded.
It is advantageous to realise the difficulties
For perseverance brings good fortune.

In a civil law case in ancient China, it was customary for the litigants to bring to court a bundle of arrows. The case is a hard one to judge, and it is only by recognising all the difficulties involved that one can find the persistence to reach a just conclusion.

In the fifth line, SIX signifies:
Biting through dried lean meat.
He receives the gold required.
Aware of danger
He perseveres without reproach.

In a criminal case, it was customary for the parties to deposit a sum in gold before the hearing. The fifth line represents the 'lord of judgment': in his powerful position he is in-inclined to be lenient, and although the case is a difficult one it is not too difficult. If the judge remains conscious of the dangers involved in making the wrong decision, his judgment will be just. The yellow of gold is the colour of correctness in the middle way.

In the sixth line, NINE signifies:
His neck is locked in the wooden cangue
His ears are gone.
Misfortune.

Deaf to good counsel, the felon is locked in the great block of the cangue, which he must carry about his neck until his crime has been expiated; it may even be that he has suffered the severest punishment of having his ears cut off.

(Right) The cangue, the Chinese equivalent of the pillory

Grace

The trigrams:
above: Ken mountain, stillness
below: Li fire, brightness

A fire breaks out from the depths of the earth, blazing up to illuminate the heavenly heights of the mountain. The outer stillness of the mountain, lit from within by the inspiration of intelligence, is the symbol of grace.

The Judgment
Pi indicates that grace, impelled by brightness, should be given a free course. Even in minor matters it is advantageous to go forward.

Commentary
The weak yin line rises between the two yang lines of the lower trigram, adorning them with its brilliance. The alteration of firmness and yielding is the pattern of heaven itself; by contemplating the patterns of heaven we begin to understand the changing seasons. As the earth adorns heaven, and heaven the earth, so do the different levels of society adorn one another, and by observing them we can learn to live in grace.

The Image
Fire below the mountain is the symbol of grace. The superior man, observing this, throws light upon the processes of government, but does not dare to intervene in the processes of law.

The Lines
In the bottom line, NINE signifies:
He adorns his feet
Leaves his carriage
And walks in grace.

He who begins in a subordinate position must learn to progress by his own labours – to 'walk on his own two feet'. He does not accept the easy assistance offered by the carriage, but at the same time he makes sure that he is properly shod for his undertaking.

In the second line, SIX signifies:
He wears his beard with elegance.

A beard is the sign of age and sagacity, and he who wishes to associate with his elders should conform to their customs. At the same time, it must be remembered that a fine beard on the chin of a young and inexperienced man is nothing but adornment, and may indicate only vanity.

In the third line, NINE signifies:
Adorned
He glistens with grace.
Righteous perseverance brings good fortune.

This is a very pleasant situation: life is good, there is every material comfort, and the phrase 'gracious living' exactly describes it. But such a state of affairs can only be maintained by perseverance in the true way.

In the fourth line, SIX signifies:
He is adorned
But only in white;
A white horse with wings.
One comes, not as a robber
But for a betrothal.

White is the colour of simplicity, but also of funerals; the winged white horse is the symbol of innocent belief, transcending the limits of time and space. The fourth line is the bottom line of the upper trigram, and finds its correlate in the bottom line of the lower trigram, from which it is separated by the strong third line. This is the 'robber', who is really a man of good reputation, anxious to ensure that the adornment of the fourth line by the first is carried out according to proper form.

In the fifth line, SIX signifies:
There is grace in hills and gardens.
His silk girdle is thin and small.
Disgrace, but in the end good fortune.

The Chinese loved gardens, and to own, or even to visit, one was a great privilege. To be invited to walk in a great man's garden, and then to appear poorly dressed, could bring nothing but humiliation and disgrace. Nevertheless, it is a relatively small fault and, even though it may be attributed to meanness rather than poverty, in the end all will be well.

In the sixth line, NINE signifies:
Nothing but grace in white.
No reproach.

At the highest stage of development, true grace is to be found without adornment. Simplicity is all.

22 PI

(Above, left) 'He is adorned, but only in white.' A detail from an eighth century representation of eight officials of the T'ang court

23 PO

Disintegration

The trigrams:

above: Ken mountain, stillness
below: K'un Earth, the passive

Po means disintegration in the sense of the breaking away of unnecessary encumbrances, and the first four lines of the hexagram symbolise a succession of losses which appear at the time to be misfortunes, but which in the long run are resolved in the fifth line, leading to recognition of virtue in the sixth.

The Judgment

Disintegration. There is no direction in which to move with advantage.

Commentary

In Po we see the weak yin lines threatening to shatter the last remaining yang lines and make it like themselves. (Po should be compared with hexagram 20, Kuan: what was a strong tower, with its two strong yang lines at the top, is now in danger of collapse, like a house with a weak ridge beam.) Small men are increasing; the superior man, therefore, remains where he is and accepts the situation. He contemplates the ebb and flow of society about him, as the tides are moved by the heavenly bodies.

The Image

The mountain stands upon the earth, and symbolises disintegration: those above can only maintain their position by strengthening those below them.

The Lines

In the bottom line, SIX signifies:

The leg of the bed is broken.
Persistence brings disaster.
Failure.

Inferior men stealthily undermining the position of the superior man; even those who remain loyal to him are threatened with misfortune. There is nothing to do but accept the situation and await its outcome.

In the second line, SIX signifies:

Po represents the autumn of 'cold dews' and 'descent of hoar frost'. This painting by Kuo Hsi (1025–1090) is entitles 'Autumn light on mountains and valleys' and it effectively portrays that time of year in which the sharp yang forms of summer continue their disintegration into the softer yin forms of approaching winter

The side of the bed is broken.
Persistence brings disaster.
Failure.

The situation deteriorates, the danger is drawing nearer. The superior man begins to mistrust even those who call themselves his friends. His only course is to adjust himself to his conditions, not to maintain his position stubbornly against those who are out to destroy him.

In the third line, SIX signifies:

He breaks with them.
No reproach.

The individual severs all his ties, both with friends and with enemies. Relying on his own integrity, he is without blame.

In the fourth line, SIX signifies:

The bed is overturned.
His skin is split:
Great misfortune.

The worst has happened: disaster has struck. The superior man is brought down, and his personal safety is threatened.

In the fifth line, SIX signifies:

A string of fishes
Symbolising favour
For the ladies of the court.
Advantage in every way.

The worst is over. Now the strong yang line in sixth place begins to exert its influence, and the yin lines submit to it, just as the empress leads her ladies in waiting like a line of fishes. The time of remaining still is past: it is advantageous to move in any direction.

In the sixth line, NINE signifies:

The largest fruit
Is uneaten on the tree.
The superior man rides in his carriage.
Inferior men throw down their houses.

On the topmost branches, the unattainable fruit grows and ripens but is not plucked: at the right time it will fall and plant a seed to grow anew. The superior man once more has influence, and he is surrounded by those who respect him, as if he rode in a carriage. But the inferior men, by their own actions, have brought destruction upon themselves.

24 FU

復

The Turning Point

The trigrams:
above: K'un Earth, the passive
below: Chen thunder and awakening

This hexagram is linked with the eleventh month, the time of the winter solstice, the turning point between a year gone and a year yet to come. The Chinese believed that natural forces, of which the thunder is the representative, rested in the earth at wintertime.

The Judgment

In Fu there is free going out and coming in, no-one to hinder. Friends arrive without blame, returning to their homes on the seventh day. Advantage in all directions.

Commentary

This hexagram indicates success, because the strong yang line is rising from the bottom, returning to its natural starting point. Motion and acceptance of motion are combined in the two trigrams making up the hexagram; that is why there is going out and coming in without hindrance. This movement, with its return after seven days, is a natural motion in accord with the movements of heaven; and the very workings of heaven and earth are represented in the return to the turning point of the year.

The Image

Thunder within the earth is the very symbol of the turning point. So, at the time of the winter solstice, the kings of old closed the passes, so that merchants and strangers were unable to travel abroad, and the kings themselves did not progress through their dominions.

The Lines

In the bottom line, NINE signifies:
Returning from a short distance:
No regrets
And great good fortune.

Small deviations from the way are often unavoidable, but he who turns back before he has gone too far, knowing the error he has made, is not to be blamed. Indeed, in acknowledging his mistake, he brings good fortune on himself.

In the second line, SIX signifies:
Turning back with heaven's blessing.
Good fortune.

All turning back requires an act of conscious decision, and wins the approbation of heaven. If one can put pride aside and follow the example of others, there will be good fortune.

In the third line, SIX signifies:
Turning back many times
Brings danger
But no reproach.

This represents those who lack constancy, who wander from the way of righteousness, turn back, and then are diverted again. There is danger that they may eventually find themselves lost in evil ways but, provided they recognise this danger, there is no blame.

In the fourth line, SIX signifies:
Walking with the others
But returning alone.

This is perhaps the hardest of all: to be associated with companions, to realise that they are going in the wrong direction and to leave them.

In the fifth line, SIX signifies:
Turning back in nobleness
Brings no remorse.

This represents a man of high principle who, recognising that he has gone astray, immediately turns back whatever it may cost him.

In the sixth line, SIX signifies:
He turns back too late.
Misfortune.
Evil causes, evil effects.
Armies sent into battle in this way
Are sure to suffer defeat
Disastrous to their emperor.
Even for ten years
There will be no redress.

When a man persists, pursuing the wrong path in blind obstinacy, there comes a point at which he cannot turn back. Nothing but disaster can ensue, and it will be a very long time before he can attempt to right matters.

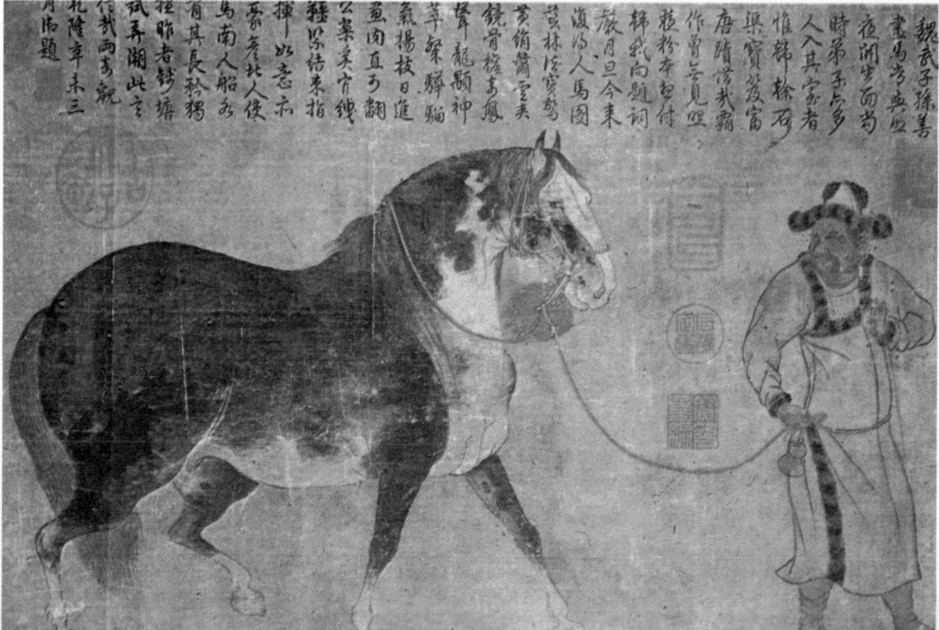

'Turning back with heaven's blessing. Good fortune.' A painting from the T'ang period

25

WU WANG

Innocence

The trigrams:

above: Ch'ien Heaven, the creative
below: Chen thunder and awakening

Wang is the symbol of recklessness and insincerity; Wu Wang comprises meanings that are almost the opposite of this. But the innocence that is symbolised is so ingenuous, so unsophisicated, that it retains one aspect of the significance of Wang – a trace of the unexpected.

The Judgment

Wu Wang indicates integrity, and resultant success. Persistence in righteousness brings its reward; but one who is not as he should be will suffer misfortune, and none of his undertakings will have a favourable outcome.

Commentary

The strong first line becomes part of an outer trigram of three yang lines, forming Ch'ien, and enclosing an inner trigram which is itself ruled by a strong line; the hexagram is full of power and movement and strength. The fifth line is a yang line, in the place of the ruler, and the weak second line responds to it: he whose movement follows the laws of heaven will be innocent and without guile.

But incorrect action on the part of the subject will lead to errors that cannot easily be put right. In what direction should he move, even though he sincerely and innocently believes in all he does? What can he achieve if it is not in accordance with the will of heaven?

The Image

The thunder rolls below the heavens, and all things find their true nature, free from all insincerity. So the kings of old, filled with virtue, made their laws according to the seasons and the ways of nature, bringing abundant nourishment to all mankind.

The Lines

In the bottom line, NINE signifies:

Protected by his innocence and his in-integrity
He achieves good fortune.

The noble impulses of the innocent heart are always good; we may follow them with confidence. But one who is devious by nature, and who justifies his actions by false appeals to honour, may flourish for a while but will suffer failure in the end.

In the second line, SIX signifies:

Count not upon the harvest while still ploughing,
Nor upon the third year's crop
Before the first is in.
It is favourable to embark upon an undertaking.

As thou sowest, so shalt thou reap; count not your chickens before they are hatched. Each task has its own time and appointed place, and, as each turns out well, so the next can be undertaken; but unwise anticipation can only bring disappointment.

In the third line, SIX signifies:

An unexpected misfortune:
An untethered cow is her master's loss,
The gain of the passer-by.

Carelessness or over-confidence is soon followed by calamity. He who innocently places his trust in the honesty of others may find himself the loser.

In the fourth line, NINE signifies:

Correct and resolute
He suffers no loss.

The open and candid man of integrity must know when to call upon his strength and resist the persuasion of others.

In the fifth line, NINE signifies:

Though he is ill
The fault is another's.
Without medicine
He will find joy in his recovery.

The difficulty in which he finds himself is not of his own making, but the result of some other's mistake. He should not try to remedy matters by external means, or experiment with some untried panacea: quietly and innocently he should let nature take its course. Then the problem will solve itself.

In the sixth line, NINE signifies:

Unplanned, out of season,
A journey can bring only misfortune.
The time is only favourable
For those with no destination in mind.

When, in any situation, the time and conditions are not right, the wisest course is to wait quietly, making no plans for the future. Trying to push ahead, opposing oneself against fate, can only result in failure.

26 TA CH'U The Restraining Force

大畜

The trigrams:

above: Ken mountain, stillness
below: Ch'ien Heaven, the creative

The creative power is subjugated to Ken, which imposes stillness. This should be contrasted with hexagram 9, Ch'u, the Power of the Weak, in which the creative power is tamed by gentleness. Here four strong lines are restrained by two weak lines, in the positions of both the prince and the minister.

The Judgment

Perseverance brings favourable results. Subsisting away from the home and family, without taking service at court, will bring good fortune. It is favourable to cross the great water.

Commentary

This hexagram symbolises strength and magnanimity, glory and honour, a daily renewal of character. The firm rises, paying respect to the worthy. Restraint in the exercise of power is praiseworthy. He who dines away from home is, by implication, entertaining other worthy people. Great and difficult undertakings, such as crossing the wide river or the sea, are successful because they accord with heaven's will.

The Image

Heaven beneath the mountain is the symbol of the restraining force of the great; at the same time we glimpse the sky among the mountain peaks. The superior man studies the sayings of antiquity and the deeds of heroes of the past, strengthening his innate virtue and learning to understand what is to come.

'Practice chariot driving and armed defence daily.' A rubbing from a clay tablet found in a Han dynasty tomb in Changtu

The Lines

In the bottom line NINE signifies:

Danger threatens.
Avoid all action.

The man who wishes to go forward boldly, but who sees that circumstances oppose him, is wise not to attempt to overcome them. Waiting patiently, he will find that the situation is bound to change.

In the second line, NINE signifies:

The springs of the wagon are broken.

There is no virtue in trying to fight the force which is holding one back. This line is central to the lower trigram, indicating that there is no blame.

In the third line, NINE signifies:

A good horse will gallop with the others.
Go forward, aware of the dangers.
Practise chariot driving and armed defence daily.
It is favourable to have a destination.

A strong horse follows the others: it is good to follow the example of a strong man. But one should still go forward cautiously, conscious of surrounding hazards and preparing oneself against unexpected attack. Above all, it is important to have a definite goal toward which one struggles.

In the fourth line, SIX signifies:

The headboard of a young bull.
Great good fortune.

In China, it was the custom to attach a board to the head of young bull, before his horns began to sprout, so that they would not be damaged, but also that they would grow in such a way that they could not do harm to others. By forestalling wild force it is most easily controlled: the safest way to deal with problems is to meet them in advance.

In the fifth line, SIX signifies:

The tusks of a gelded boar.
Good fortune.

The strength of forward advance is now even more impetuous, likened to the charge of a savage boar. But if the nature of the boar is changed by gelding, his tusks are no longer a danger. This is a more indirect and subtle way of meeting danger in advance.

In the sixth line, NINE signifies:

Reaching command of heaven.
Success.

There are no more obstructions: the creative power throws off the weight of the mountain. Following the way of heaven, honoured by all, the wise man achieves all that he desires and nothing stands in his way.

Nourishment

The trigrams:

above: Ken mountain, stillness
below: Chen thunder and awakening

The form of this hexagram is readily seen as a picture of a mouth wide open to receive sustenance. The lower three lines represent nourishment of oneself, and the upper trigram represents the nourishment of others, more particularly nourishment in a spiritual sense.

The Judgment

I indicates that perseverance brings good fortune. Pay heed to those who nourish others, and observe how they seek to nourish themselves.

Commentary

Take and give the right kind of nourishment, and good fortune is assured. Observe the needs of others, both those who nourish themselves and those whom you would wish to nourish, but do not neglect your own sustenance. As heaven and earth nourish all things, so the wise man nourishes men of talent and virtue, and through them reaches out to all the people, nourishing them both physically and spiritually.

There is a reference here to the words of Meng-tse (c. 371-288 BC): 'One who nourishes his smaller self becomes a small man, and one who nourishes his greater self becomes a great man . . . The man who only eats and drinks is counted mean by others, for he nourishes what is little to the neglect of what is great.'

The Image

Below the mountain the thunder rolls, the image of nourishing. The superior man is careful of everything that he says, and he observes due moderation in his eating and drinking.

The Lines

In the bottom line, NINE signifies:

You let your magic tortoise go.
Your mouth hangs open.
Misfortune.

The tortoise was regarded as a magic animal because it appeared to live on air and required no earthly sustenance; the shells of tortoises were used for divination. The man with his mouth agape may be taken as symbolising either personal greed or envy of others: he has abandoned his self-reliance for empty discontent and jealousy of those who find themselves in better circumstances than himself.

In the second line, SIX signifies:

Turning from the path
To seek nourishment in the high hills.
Persisting in such ways brings misfortune.

Here the man has sought sustenance from those in high places, living on the charity of others. In this, he behaves unworthily, succeeding only in bringing misfortune upon himself.

In the third line, SIX signifies:

Nourishment that nourishes not
Brings great misfortune.
Avoid such ways for ten years
For there is no favourable destination.

Wandering from gratification to gratification brings no satisfaction. Ten years is a complete cycle of time, and signifies forever. Seeking nourishment in this way is like taking no nourishment at all; the lord Buddha gave up sustenance on the advice of his teachers, and soon came to regret such an empty method of self discipline.

In the fourth line, SIX signifies:

Good fortune comes
From seeking nourishment in the high hills.
Staring about with hungry eyes like a tiger
Brings no reproach.

At first this seems to contradict the second line, but we have now reached the upper trigram, and the line no longer refers to a man bent on seeking his own advantage but to one who searches about him for others to help him attain his high ideal.

In the fifth line, SIX signifies:

Turning away from the path.
Perseverance brings good fortune.
But success does not lie in crossing the great water.

Here is a man conscious that his own nourishment is not complete: to continue his nourishment of others he must seek help in developing his own strength. Now is not the time for him to embark on any great undertaking, for he is still dependent upon the assistance of others.

In the sixth line, NINE signifies:,

The fountain of nourishment.
Watching for dangers brings good fortune.
Now is the time to cross the great water.

This describes one who has become at last a great sage, with a profound influence upon spiritual sustenance of others. Such a man, who takes note of all the pitfalls that surround and remains conxcious of the responsibilities, can undertake the most difficult labours.

27 I

'Staring about with hungry eyes like a tiger . . .'

28 TA KUO

大過

Excess

The trigrams:

above: Tui a pool of water, joy
below: Sun wind, gentleness, penetration

In this hexagram the four strong lines are held from without by two weak lines. Where the strong holds the weak all is well and nothing is out of balance, but here the reverse is the case. The hexagram is like a beam, thick and heavy in the middle, but weak at its ends.

The Judgment

The weight is excessive. The ridgepole of the roof sags and is near to breaking point. It is favourable to have a destination.

Commentary

This is a condition that cannot last: the weight of the strong lines is too much for the weak ones. The situation must be changed: an extraordinary state of affairs demands extraordinary measures to deal with it. But although the tasks to be carried out are great, nothing is to be gained by violent movement. The gentle penetration of the wind is the example to follow, and full consideration should be given to the direction in which the desired change is to be made.

The Image

The forest is submerged in the water, the pool rises above it. The superior man, though he stands alone, is free from fear; if he has to withdraw from the world he is undaunted.

The Lines

In the bottom line, SIX signifies:

Spread white rushes upon the floor.
No error.

If the roof is to be lowered, then a mat of rushes should be spread to take the weight. White rushes are much rarer than ordinary ones, signifying the care of a valuable object, and due caution in planning for its preservation.

In the second line, NINE signifies:

The withered tree sprouts from its roots.
An old man takes a young wife.
Everything is favourable.

The old tree standing in the water puts forth new shoots: an unusual symbol of a rare re-awakening. This is the situation when an old man takes a new young wife, but in this case all is well.

In the third line, NINE signifies:

The ridgepole sags.
Misfortune.

This refers to a man who insists on driving ahead, taking no advice from others, and trying to force his companions to go along with him. Resenting this, they refuse to give him their support: the burden steadily increases, and catastrophe is the only outcome.

In the fourth line, NINE signifies:

The ridgepole is shored up.
Good fortune.
But if there is insincerity
Humiliation.

A leader emerges who, by his good relations with those of lower rank, succeeds in becoming master of the situation. But if he does not work for the good of all, misusing his position for personal advancement, nothing but disgrace will ensue.

In the fifth line, NINE signifies:

The withered tree puts forth flowers.
An old woman takes a young husband.
No blame. No praise.

Blossoming, the old tree exhausts its powers and only brings its death nearer. An old woman may marry again, but she is barren and no children will result. There is no evil in such a situation, but equally no successful outcome.

In the sixth line, SIX signifies:

Wading through the water
It rose above his head.
Misfortune, but no blame.

Here the man goes forward courageously, trying to complete his task whatever the danger. But although he meets with misfortune the fault is not his, and he is not to blame.

(Above) 'The withered tree puts forth flowers'. A painting on silk by an anonymous artist of the Ch'ing epoch

29 K'AN

The Abyss

The trigrams:

above: K'an dangerous deep water
below: K'an dangerous deep water

This is one of only eight hexagrams in which the trigram is doubled. In each trigram a strong yang line has plunged into the deep between two yin lines, and is closed in by them, as deep water lies in a ravine. The trigram K'an represents the soul of man enclosed within the body, the light of human reason locked up in the dark of animal instinct.

The Judgment

Abyss upon abyss, danger piled on danger. But if you are sincere there is success locked up within you, and whatever you undertake will be successful.

Commentary

There is grave danger, but, as water flows without flooding over, so a man can cross the abyss without loss of confidence. Employing his reason he will succeed, and setting his eye upon a goal to be attained he will win respect and achieve results. The dangers sent from heaven none can escape, but earthly dangers are but mountains, rivers, hills and precipices. So, too, are the ominous means that are employed by kings and princes to protect their realms, both from without and within.

The Image

The water flows ever on and so reaches its destination: the image of the abyss upon the abyss. So the superior man walks in eternal virtue, instructing others in the conduct of affairs.

The Lines

In the bottom line, SIX signifies:

Abyss upon abyss.
He falls into the depths.
Misfortune.

Growing accustomed to danger, a man can become hardened to it, and his familiarity may turn to evil ways. He is bound to be caught, and misfortune is the natural result of his error.

In the second line, NINE signifies:

The abyss is dangerous and deep.
Taking small steps
He only slowly climbs out.

Beset by dangers, one cannot quickly overcome them. It is best first to become accustomed to the situation and then, by gradual means, to overcome it. A spring at first flows slowly, moving forward and gathering its strength until it flows out into the open.

In the third line, SIX signifies:

Forward and backward, abyss beneath abyss.
He falls deeper into the pit
Unable to help himself.

Any attempt to escape from the danger only increases it, and escape is impossible. Wasting one's energies on fruitless attempts, one finds oneself in greater danger.

In the fourth line, SIX signifies:

A flagon of wine
And with it a bowl of rice
Handed in through a hole in the rock.
There is certainly no blame.

Help is at hand, but although the fault is not one's own, very little can be done about it. The available relief is rough and ready, for this is not the time to stand on ceremony.

In the fifth line, NINE signifies;

The water does not overflow the abyss,
Rising only to the brim.
There is no blame.

The way out of danger is to follow the line of least resistance, as the water flows away out of the ravine. In normal times a man might give thought to what he was doing, carefully considering every step: in great danger it is enough to escape from it by any means.

In the sixth line, SIX signifies:

Bound with black ropes
Hedged in by thorns
For three years he cannot find the way.
Great misfortune.

Here is a man so hemmed in by danger that he cannot find any way out of it. But although his perilous situation will persist, it is finite, and he can plan for his eventual release.

30 LI

離

Flaming beauty

The trigrams:
above: Li fire, brightness, beauty
below: Li fire, brightness, beauty

This is another doubled hexagram. The trigram Li means both 'clinging. and 'brightness', as the flame clings burning bright, with no certain form of its own except as it is defined by the object on which it burns. Where K'an represents the soul shut up within the darkness of the body, Li represents the radiant beauty of nature.

The Judgment

Li is the clinging flame. Persistence brings great good fortune. Nurturing cows brings rewards and blessings.

The cow is the symbol of docility, indicating that the wise man submits to the will of heaven. One should make oneself as dependent upon the principle of righteousness as animals are upon nature.

Commentary

The sun and moon depend from heaven, as living things depend upon earth. Clear bright consciousness of what is right results in the transforming and perfecting of all things under heaven. The weak yin lines in the second and fifth positions between the strong yang lines indicate success and the fact that docility like that of a cow will lead to good fortune.

The Image

Fire rises in two tongues of flaming beauty. So the wise man sheds his light over every quarter of the earth.

The Lines

In the bottom line, NINE signifies:
First light: tracks run in all directions.
But approaching with respectful steps
He suffers no blame.

As day dawns, people awake and, still sleepy, may set off in the wrong direction. But one who remains calm can accommodate all the different impressions that flood into his newly awakened consciousness, and set about his tasks without confusion.

In the second line, SIX signifies:
Bright yellow sunlight.
Great good fortune.

It is now full daylight. Yellow is the colour of moderation; in China it was the prerogative of the upper classes, often being reserved for the royal family and the highest nobles. The middle way, the golden mean, brings success.

In the third line, NINE signifies:
In the light of the setting sun
He does not strike his *ch'ing* and sing
But mourns his lost youth.
Misfortune.

The *ch'ing* is a stone chime which, struck with a heavy stick, produced a musical note. As Meng-tse said: 'A concert is complete when the large bell proclaims the commencement of the music, and the ringing stone proclaims its close.' At the end of the day, the man who does not celebrate the pleasure of his past life, and what is still to come, will bring only sadness and misfortune upon himself.

In the fourth line, NINE signifies:
It comes so suddenly,
Flames up, dies, and is cast away.

A man who rises suddenly to success will as suddenly vanish again from view. Unexpected good fortune may burst upon us, but it will have passed away before we have had time to enjoy it. Real success comes slowly.

In the fifth line, SIX signifies:
His tears flow in torrents
He groans in sorrow.
Good fortune.

Here the man has reached the high point of his life: at last understanding the vanity of all things, he reviews his situation and soberly regrets whatever he had done wrong in the past.

In the sixth line, NINE signifies:
The king sends him forth
To punish and set things right.
Victorious, he kills the rebel leader
But takes his followers captive.
No reproach.

Punishment should not be distributed indiscriminately. In public life, revolution is best treated by rooting out evil in the person of the rebel leader, but sparing the followers. In the spiritual life, the same moderation should apply.

(Above) Meng-tse, otherwise known as Mencius. He was a disciple of Confucian doctrine who believed in the essential goodness of human nature

Influence

The trigrams:
above: Tui a pool of water, joy
below: Ken mountain, stillness

Ken, the lower trigram, represents the youngest son; Tui, the upper, represents the youngest daughter. Thus this hexagram signifies the persuasive influence that exists between the sexes, representing wooing and marriage.

The Judgment
Influence, attraction, success. Righteous perseverance furthers one's desires. Taking a maiden for a wife brings good fortune.

Commentary
The yielding trigram Tui is above, the firm trigram Ken is below. Although they are opposite in nature, their mutual attraction draws them together. In many of the most auspicious of Taoist positions for sexual intercourse the man is below the woman. All nature owes its existence to the influence of earth upon heaven, and heaven upon earth. In the same way, the wise man exerts his influence upon men's hearts, observing what causes them pleasure and what causes pain, and bringing the whole world to peace.

The Image
The lake is high upon the mountain. So the superior man welcomes those who approach him, humbly and without selfishness.

The Lines
In the bottom line, SIX signifies:
He feels the influence in his big toe.

Even before a man begins to move, he reveals his activity in a flexing of the toes of his foot, but this intention is not apparent to others. As long as it has no visible outcome, it has no importance to the rest of the world, and is neither good nor evil.

In the second line, SIX signifies:
The influence shows itself in the legs.
Misfortune.
It is better not to venture forth.

An ill thought-out movement, a sudden movement of the legs, may easily result in a fall. It is better to remain where one is until the persuasive influence is analysed and understood.

In the third line, NINE signifies:
He feels the influence in his loins.
Clinging to his wife in this way
Is shameful.

Here is a man who follows the dictates of his heart or of his animal instincts rather than of his head.

In the fourth line, NINE signifies:
Righteous perseverance brings good fortune.
There are no regrets.
But when a man is agitated in mind,
His thoughts flying to and fro,
Only his closest friends
Will be influenced by him.

The influence to move comes from within; there are no regrets at having delayed until the moment is right. But the man who acts without due consideration will find it difficult to persuade more than his nearest companions to follow him.

In the fifth line, NINE signifies:
The influence is felt in the nape of the neck.
No regrets.

Resolution shows itself in a stiffening of the back and the neck. But even though the man will experience no remorse at this strengthening of his resolve, he may still find it difficult to persuade others.

In the sixth line, SIX signifies:
The influence shows itself in the jaws and tongue.

Trying to persuade others by talk alone is a superficial way of doing things, particularly if there is no profound thought behind what is said. Its influence is of little importance, bringing neither good nor bad fortune.

31 HSIEN

'The yielding Tui is above, the firm Ken below.' A nineteenth century album painting representing the union of yin and yang

32 HENG

Endurance

The trigrams:

above: Chen thunder and awakening
below: Sun wind, gentleness, penetration

This hexagram, with the strong trigram Chen above the weak trigram Sun, is the exact inverse of Hsien, the preceding hexagram, and represents the bonds of an enduring marriage.

The Judgment

Endurance signifies steady progress, with success and freedom from error. Righteous persistence brings its reward; and it is certainly favourable to have a destination in view.

Commentary

Thunder and wind work together, representing gentleness combined with arousal. The interplay of strong and weak lines makes for endurance, and success, freedom from error and the rewards of righteous persistence all indicate that the established way can be pursued for a long time; for the way, as it is followed by heaven and earth, sun and moon, endures for ever, and the four seasons, continuing their ceaseless cycle of transformation, extend their influence for eternity. The wise man keeps steadfastly to his chosen path, succeeding in transforming all things under heaven and rendering them perfect. The true nature of everything in heaven and earth can be discovered in contemplating what it is that makes them endure.

The Image

Thunder and wind, the one influencing the other, are the image of endurance. The superior man stands firm, his direction unaltered.

The Lines

In the bottom line, SIX signifies:

Lasting success is not attained hastily
By digging a burrow for oneself.
Persistence in this course brings misfortune,
For one is without destination.

Whatever is to endure must be developed slowly, and after careful consideration. The man who attempts to establish a lasting position by entrenching himself in his present circumstances shows no thought for the future, or for the direction in which he should go.

In the second line, NINE signifies:

There are no regrets.

Although forward movement is necessary, one should avoid taking action before the time is ripe. To preserve the continuity of one's life, it is important to hold to one's principles. The man who realises that he is not yet ready, who does not attempt anything beyond his present powers, will have no regrets.

In the third line, NINE signifies:

Lacking persistence in his virtuous conduct
He meets with disgrace
And lasting humiliation.

A man who changes with the wind, leaving his emotions at the mercy of what happens in the world around him, sacrifices the inner endurance of his character. Friends and supporters will desert him, and he will end his life in shame.

In the fourth line, NINE signifies:

There is no quarry in the field.

Persistence itself is not enough. A man who takes his bow to the field, hunting where there is no game to be shot at, is foolish. In the same way, the trader who persists in attempts to sell where there are no customers, the politician who speaks without an audience, the general who pursues a non-existent foe, is not seeking out his true goal.

In the fifth line, SIX signifies:

Obstinate constancy is favourable for a woman
But not for a man.

The Chinese held that a wife should follow her man for the whole of her life; but a man should decide upon his duty as the circumstances determined it. Adhering blindly to tradition and conformity, he loses sight of his ultimate destination.

In the sixth line, SIX signifies:

Persisting in ceaseless activity
Brings misfortune.

Impatience is as much to be deplored as conservatism, for insisting upon immediate action a man will not give himself time to see and avoid errors into which he is hurrying himself. Headstrong endurance can only lead to misfortune.

Withdrawal

The trigrams:

above: Ch'ien Heaven, the creative
below: Ken mountain, stillness

The dark power of Ken rises from below, and the spiritual light retreats before it to safety. This hexagram is associated with the sixth month of the year, in which the power of the sun first begins to decline before the power of winter. So retreat is not a matter to be decided wilfully by man, but a natural process, and withdrawal in these circumstances is proper.

The Judgment

Withdrawal means success. Persistence in small matters is nevertheless to one's advantage.

Commentary

In certain situations a retreat is in effect an advance. A strong yang line is in the fifth place, the place of the ruler, and all the other lines respond to it: all actions take place in accordance with the times. As young plants grow when properly watered, so persistence in small matters brings advantage. A withwithdrawal at the proper time presages success.

The Image

The mountain stands below heaven. The superior man, keeping his distance from men of inferior character, is not angry but dignified.

The Lines

In the bottom line, SIX signifies:

Withdrawing with the rearguard.
This is dangerous.
It is no time to choose a destination.

The rearguard of a retreating army is designed for sacrifice: few survive. It is obviously better to be in the van; but whatever one's position, there is no time, in the disorder of a retreat, to seek out a direction of one's own.

In the second line, SIX signifies:

He binds him with yellow rawhide thongs.
None can untie them.

Yellow is the colour of the middle way, the correct line of duty; and rawhide thongs are very strong and not to be torn or unknotted. With a powerful will, the inferior man is bound to the superior, so that he cannot be shaken loose; in this way he intends to achieve his goal.

In the third line, NINE signifies:

Delay in withdrawal
Is frightening and dangerous.
But retaining the servants and concubines
Brings good fortune.

It is the retainers and their lack of initiative that occasions the delay, and the most obvious course is to abandon them to their fate. But the superior man who engages them in his service, taking the initiative and leading them out of danger, has made a step in the right direction.

In the fourth line, NINE signifies:

Choosing withdrawal, the superior man benefits,
But the inferior man is destroyed.

The man who makes a calculated retreat from a dangerous situation, not allowing himself to be burdened with an inferior, escapes; but the inferior man, deprived of the counsel of the other, will suffer great misfortune. The wise man is not to be blamed for this; he is not compelled to link his fate with that of another.

In the fifth line, NINE signifies:

Withdrawal by agreement.
Perseverance brings good fortune.

When the time is right for retreat, the wise man recognises it, and there is no need for discussion and disagreement. But he must still adhere firmly to his decision, modifying it only as circumstances change.

In the sixth line, NINE signifies:

Happy withdrawal.
Everything is favourable.

The sense of the word 'withdrawal' is now subtly altered, for there is no further danger in retreat. The superior man has reached a spiritual state free from doubt, and there are now no obstacles to his retiring from the world into contemplation.

33 TUN

'A Taoist temple in the mountains' by the tenth century painter Dong Yuan. The hexagram Tun is associated with the sixth month of the year, when the mists begin to form after the days of high summer

34 TA CHUANG

大壯

Strength of Greatness

The trigrams:

above: Chen thunder and awakening
below: Ch'ien Heaven, the creative

The four strong yang lines have entered from below and are ascending; the combination of the strength of Ch'ien with the powerful movement of Chen is what gives meaning to the name of this hexagram. In appearance it is reminiscent of the horned head of the goat, an animal renowned for rapid powerful movement. The hexagram is also linked with the second month of the Chinese year. the time when everything is springing strongly to life.

The Judgment

Ta Chuang is the strength of the great. Perseverance in a course of righteousness brings reward.

Commentary

The strength of righteousness and greatness combined brings full understanding of the inner nature of everything in heaven and on earth. The lower trigram, signifying strength, controls the upper, which signifies movement, and from this results great vigour. Righteous persistence is duly rewarded because, in the context of this hexagram, what is great and what is right are synonymous.

The Image

Thunder above the heavens is the image of the strength of greatness. The superior man does not lead a path that is not in accord with established order.

The Lines

In the bottom line, NINE signifies:

Strength in the toes.
But going forward brings misfortune,
This is certainly true.
Have confidence.

The feet are the lowest part of the body, and furthest from the brain. Trying to advance by sheer brute strength, like someone who possesses ambition but no intelligence, is bound to lead to disaster. The wise man restrains his violent impulses, but retains confidence in his future advancement.

In the second line, NINE signifies:

Righteous persistence brings good fortune.

There are now opportunities for advancement, but it is wise still not to plunge unheedingly ahead. Only by maintaining the true inner equilibrium of Tao, without excessive use of strength, is good fortune achieved.

In the third line, NINE signifies:

The inferior man exploits his strength
But the superior man is restrained,
For persistence is dangerous:
The goat butts obstinately against the hedge
And his horns are caught.

The inferior man who comes to power glories in it and abuses it, but the wise man is conscious at all times of the danger inherent in thrusting ahead regardless of circumstances; he will renounce or limit his power when there is no purpose in an empty display of strength.

In the fourth line, NINE signifies:

Righteous persistence brings good fortune,
Regrets vanish.
The hedge falls apart,
The goat frees himself.
In a big wagon, the axle is very strong.

Obstacles are best overcome by calm and intelligent perseverance. The goat does not

free himself by fruitless struggling, but by slowly working his horns free from the branches as they part. The power of the superior man does not show itself openly but, as the wagon is borne forward dependent entirely upon the strength of its axle, so he is able to bear the great load of his responsibilities.

In the fifth line, SIX signifies:

> The goat is lost too easily
> But there is no cause for regret.

The goat is renowned for its outward aggressiveness and its inward docility. The situation has been resolved, perhaps too easily, so that one gives up the struggle to rest; nevertheless, abandoning one's obstinate position at this point will bring no misfortune.

In the sixth line, SIX signifies:

> The goat butts obstinately against the hedge
> There is no advantage in going on,
> But taking due note of the mistake
> Brings good fortune.

Going too far, one comes to a deadlock, in which it is impossible to advance or retreat. The more one struggles, the more one is ensnared. But by coming to an understanding of the obstacle one is enabled to find the solution.

'The goat butts obstinately . . .' From a thirteenth century scroll by Chao Meng-fu

35 CHIN

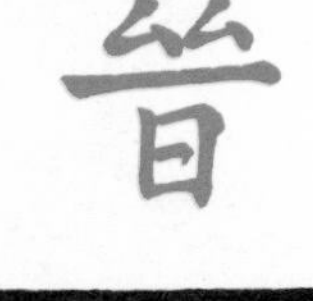

(Above) *'The great prince is honoured with many horses . . .' A gift of horses for the emperor Ch'ien-lung*

Progress

The trigrams:
above: Li fire, brightness, beauty
below: K'un Earth, the passive

This hexagram represents the sun rising over the earth, a symbol of steady and unimpeded progress.

The Judgment

The great prince is honoured with many horses, and in a single day the emperor grants him three audiences.

Commentary

The Chinese character Chin itself means progress. The combination of the passive trigram K'un with the beauty of Li represents the earth radiant with bright light. The weak yin lines ascend to the fifth and ruling line of the hexagram, signifying a great prince, splendid steeds, and royal favour.

The effect of progress comes from the prince, a man subservient to his emperor but at the same time a leader of others. He does not abuse his influence, but dedicates it to the service of his ruler who, enlightened and free from jealousy, showers favours upon him.

The Image

Chin is the image of progress, the sun rising above the earth. The superior man reflects in himself the brightness of heavenly virtue.

The Lines

In the bottom line, SIX signifies:
Going forward, then hindered;
But persistence brings good fortune.
He meets lack of confidence with tranquillity.
No error.

Even when everything seems to be going forward, one may be brought to a halt by influences over which one has no control. It may be that those with whom one is dealing have no confidence in oneself; but the only wise course is not to attempt to arouse confidence, or try to force one's way forward, but to remain cheerfully untroubled by the delay.

In the second line, SIX signifies:
Progress in sorrow.
Persistence brings good fortune.
And great happiness comes
From the honoured grandmother.

The sorrow arises from the fact that the progress envisaged receives no recognition; but there is no alternative to perseverance, even though present circumstances bring nothing but unhappiness, for in due course someone, man or woman, will bestow gentle affection and instruction.

In the third line, SIX signifies:
All are in accord.
Sorrow vanishes.

This is the moment at which one realises that one is making true progress, for the backing of others is encouraging.

In the fourth line, NINE signifies:
Making progress like a squirrel.
Persistence is dangerous.

The squirrel builds up large stores of food; some of them are in places that the squirrel subsequently forgets. The squirrel in a cage constantly runs forward on its wheel, making for a destination that it can never reach. So the man who amasses great possessions (often by dubious means) seems to have a goal in view but seldom reaches it, and often loses not only his gains but everything that he has.

In the fifth line, SIX signifies:
All sorrow vanishes.
Care not for loss or gain.
It is advantageous to have a destination.
All things are favourable.

A man who finds himself in an important position in an era of progress should keep himself gentle and impassive, and not regret any past mistakes. He should look forward in confidence that all his ventures will succeed.

In the sixth line, NINE signifies:
He butts onward with lowered horns
Only to subdue his own people.
Consciousness of his danger
Brings no blame.
But persistence results in humiliation.

Making progress by means of attack is only permissible in a situation where it is necessary to correct the mistakes of one's own followers; but to pursue punishment for its own sake is a sign of a lack of enlightenment. One who remains aware of the danger he risks is able to avoid mistakes, however, and succeed in what he set out to do; perseverance in aggressive behaviour can only lead to shame and misfortune.

Sinking Light

The trigrams:
above: K'un Earth, the passive
below: Li fire, brightness, beauty

The sun has sunk beneath the earth: the name of the hexagram, Ming I, literally means 'wounding of the bright'. This hexagram comprises not only a transposition of the trigrams of the previous hexagram, but is in fact its inversion. In Chin, a wise man, assisted by competent helpers, made steady progress; in Ming I, the wise man is in peril from a malevolent man in authority.

The Judgment
The light is sinking. Righteous persistence in the face of adversity brings advancement.

Commentary
As the sun declines into the earth, so its light is extinguished. Meet adversity like King Wen, attiring your inner self in refinement and intelligence, displaying gentleness and compliance in your outward behaviour. Determined to triumph over all difficulties, hide your light under a bushel. Be like Prince Chi who, with his troubles locked within his heart, fixed his whole being upon righteousness with rigid determination.

The Image
The light sinks into the earth, the image of Ming I. The superior man, walking among the people, keeps his light hidden. But still it shines.

The Lines
In the bottom line, NINE signifies:

The light sinks as he flies through the sky
His wings droop.
For three days, busy about his occasions,
The superior man goes without food or rest.
Though his lord whispers about it,
He has a goal in view.

The Emperor Yü, busied with the problems of controlling the floods, frequently passed the door of his family home without stopping to greet his relations; Confucius himself is reported to have gone several days without stopping for food. Nevertheless, one who concerns himself too much with mundane matters will be forced to withdraw from obstacles too great to be surmounted. In spite of everything, however, if he has a true goal in view, he will be honoured, even though those above him in authority criticise him for persistence.

In the second line, SIX signifies:

The light sinks.
Wounded in the thigh,
He saves himself by the strength of a horse.
And brings assistance.
Good fortune.

Though the superior man conceals his light, he is harmed by the actions of one in authority. But striving with all his strength, he brings relief to the distress of others in a similar plight.

In the third line, NINE signifies:

The light sinks
As he searches in the south
And captures the prince of darkness.
But foolish persistence must be avoided.

By good chance, and not by design, the wise man encounters and vanquishes his principal enemy. But, no matter how good his intentions and right his cause, he was vulnerable and showed excessive zeal that amounted almost to madness. Though it is praiseworthy to struggle against adversity. it is foolish to endanger oneself unnecessarily.

In the fourth line, SIX signifies:

Leaving his gate and courtyard,
He thrusts into the left of the belly
And exposes the heart
Of the prince of darkness.

The wise man has exposed the true nature of his adversary. But, performing this deed as he sets out from his place of safety, and realising that the evil is too great to cope with, he withdraws even further from the scene.

In the fifth line, SIX signifies:

The light sinks.
As it sank for Prince Chi.
But righteous persistence is rewarded.

Prince Chi lived at the court of the tyrant Ti-Hsin, who is clearly the 'prince of darkness' referred to. But although Prince Chi could not withdraw physically from the court, he hid his true feelings and feigned insanity. Treated as little more than a slave, he did not allow his misery to deflect him from his belief that the true light can never be extinguished.

In the sixth line, SIX signifies:

No light in the darkness.
After ascending to the heavens
He plunged into the depths of earth.

The prince of darkness is triumphant. But the darkness brings its own destruction, and in the end evil will be overcome.

36 MING I

The emperor Yü sometimes known as 'the engineer': he is traditionally credited with having confined the rivers of China within their banks after thirty years of labour

37 CHIA JEN

家人

The Family

The trigrams:

above: Sun — wind, gentleness, penetration
below: Li — fire, brightness, beauty

This hexagram represents the strength of the family. The strong yang line at the top represents the father, the strong bottom line the son. The strong line in the fifth place may also represent the father, the weak yin line in second place the wife: alternatively, the strong lines in fifth and third place are two brothers, the weak second and fourth lines their wives. Each individual line possesses the character in accordance with its position.

The Judgment

It is the woman's persistence that brings good fortune. Women who cast this hexagram should take it as a favourable omen, but for men it does not have a successful significance.

Commentary

It is the place of women to keep within; men stand without. Keeping to their appointed places, men and women act in accordance with the laws of heaven; when the family is in order, then all the social relationships of mankind are also in order. When father, mother, sons and brothers take their proper positions within the structure of the family, when husbands play their proper part and wives are truly wifely, all is well.

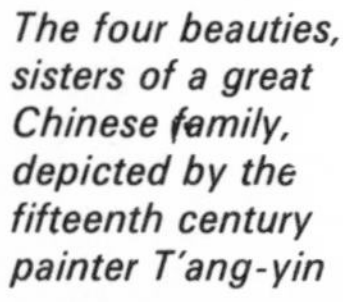

The four beauties, sisters of a great Chinese family, depicted by the fifteenth century painter T'ang-yin

The Image

The wind rises from the fire. The words of the superior man are full of meaning, his life is constant and endures.

The Lines

In the bottom line, NINE signifies:

The family circle is closed
And in good order.
Regret vanishes.

The family is a well-defined unit, and every member knows his place. From his earliest years, each child must be treated with kind and loving firmness, so that he learns discipline; if he is allowed to exercise his whims and passions, he and his parents will eventually regret the indulgence.

In the second line, SIX signifies:

She should not indulge her whims
But attend to the needs of the household.
Peristence brings good fortune.

Although this line refers directly to the position of a wife in the home, it has a much wider application. One who is in a position of service, whether to a single household or to the state, should not follow his own selfish desires but should devote himself to his proper duties.

In the third line, NINE signifies:

When there are quarrels in the family
Too much strictness brings regret,
But nevertheless good fortune.
When women and children mock,
Disgrace.

Discipline tempered with tenderness is the best means of preserving concord, and too great severity is to be avoided; nevertheless, in case of doubt, strictness is to be preferred to indulgence, and brings happiness.

In the fourth line, SIX signifies:

She is the treasure of the house.
Great good fortune.

The fourth line represents the daughter-in-law, who can prove to be the greatest treasure of the family, but this verse also refers to any woman of the house who nourishes the family and supervises its economy. The fourth line can also represent the faithful minister of a kingdom.

In the fifth line, NINE signifies:

He is a king in his own house.
Fear not;
Good fortune.

When a husband governs his family as a king governs his kingdom (or conversely) all is well. Ruling justly and kindly, evoking love and banishing fear, he brings prosperity to all.

In the sixth line, NINE signifies:

His sincerity and confidence
Bring him honour.
Good fortune in the end.

The man who subjects his actions to constant self-examination will bring good fortune to himself and to all his dependants, earning himself honour and universal acclaim.

Opposites

The trigrams:
above: Lui fire, brightness, beauty
below: Tui a pool of water, joy

Li, the flame, burns upward, while Tui, the pool of water, soaks downward – two movements that are opposite to one another. Moreover, Li represents the second daughter and Tui the youngest daughter: though they may live in the same house their attentions are directed to two different men, and therefore their desires will run in opposite directions.

The Judgment
Opposites – but in small matters, good fortune.

Commentary
Fire moves upward, water moves downward, like two women under one roof whose wills do not accord. But if joy is joined to beauty, there is radiance. The weak yin lines ascend, responding to the strong yang lines and indicating good fortune in minor matters. For, although heaven and earth may be separate and apart, they work to the same end; men and women are opposite, but they desire union; all things are individual, but each accomplishes its purpose in accordance with its kind.

The Image
Fire above, and the pool below: the image of K'uei. The superior man remains himself, even in the midst of the crowd.

The Lines
In the bottom line, NINE signifies:
There are no regrets.
He loses his horse, but should not run after it.
For it will return of itself.
Meeting with evil men
He avoids condemnation.

When a man begins to encounter opposition, he should not attempt to bring about reconciliation by force, for he will only evoke greater opposition; just as a horse that is pursued will continue to run ever further away. With evil men, one should be particularly cautious: it is impossible to dismiss them forcibly, or ignore them, and so one should endure their company until they leave of their own accord.

In the second line, NINE signifies:
He meets his lord in a narrow street.
No blame.

This is an accidental encounter, possibly between people who have not been on speaking terms for some time; but, the street being narrow, there is no way in which they can avoid one another, and so friendly relations are re-established.

In the third line, SIX signifies:
He sees his wagon halted,
The oxen reined back.
His hair and his nose are cut off.
An ominous beginning
But an auspicious end.

Everything is going wrong: there are obstacles at every turn. One is hindered and dragged back, insulted and dishonoured in the most terrible way. K'uei is different by only the second line from hexagram 21, Shih Ho, 'biting through'; and the texts of the third and fifth lines of K'uei are reminiscent of the texts of Shih Ho, and clearly have a related significance.

In the fourth line, NINE signifies:
Solitary and estranged
One meets a like-minded person
With whom to live in confidence.
There is danger, but no mistake.

Holding oneself aloof from the crowd because one cannot agree with their standards and beliefs, one becomes lonely. One is then particularly vulnerable, and an encounter with someone who seems to share one's isolation can assume an exaggerated significance. However, if one is aware of the dangers inherent in the situation it can be turned to the best advantage and there will be no regrets.

In the fifth line, SIX signifies:
Regrets vanish.
He cleaves to his companion
As if he bit through the thin skin.
Going forward,
What error can there be in this?

At first, one does not recognise the true friend; then it is as if a veil had been torn away. One should go forward to meet such a friend; all obstacles will be removed.

In the sixth line, NINE signifies:
Wandering solitary and estranged
He sees a pig caked with mud,
A wagonload of devils.
First he draws his bow against them,
Then lays it aside;
For this is no assailant
But a close relative.
He goes forward in soft rain;
Good fortune comes.

Here one has kept oneself aloof so long that one cannot recognise one's true friends: they appear as treacherous and unclean as a pig in his sty, or as menacing as a wagon full of devils. One's first reaction is to defend oneself; only in due course does one realise that the apparent enemy is in reality a friend. As the soft rain of summer cleans dirt and dust from everything, so one's doubts are swept away and one advances toward a successful outcome. This text is often quoted as an example of the obscurity of the I Ching.

38 K'UEI

39 CHIEN

Obstacles

The trigrams:

above: K'an water, dangerous pit
below: Ken mountain, stillness

This hexagram represents a perilous abyss in front, with a precipitous mountain rising behind. Whichever way one turns one is beset with obstacles.

The Judgment

There is advantage to the south and west; obstacles to the north and east. It is advantageous to see and meet with a great man. Righteous persistence brings good fortune.

Commentary

Chien denotes difficulty, for danger lies in front of one. Wisdom lies in perceiving the danger and successfully avoiding it: the southwest is the direction of retreat, and that way leads to the middle course, but the northeast is the direction of advance, and nothing favourable lies that way. The strong yang line in the fifth position indicates that righteous persistence will be of great value to the community or the state; visiting a great man is bound to result in significant achievements.

The Image

Water upon the mountain, the image of Chien. So the superior man turns back in order to examine himself and cultivate his virtue.

The Lines

In the bottom line, SIX signifies:

Going forward means obstacles,
Standing still earns praise.

Encountering obstacles, threatened with danger, one should not attempt to go blindly forward; one should consider the nature of the obstacles and how to deal with them.

In the second line, SIX signifies:

The servant of the king
Encounters obstacle after obstacle,
But the fault is not his.

This is the path of duty: when a man may not act upon his own responsibility but must continue to struggle in the service of others, or for a higher cause, then he should not be reproached.

In the third line, NINE signifies:

Going forward leads only to obstacles
And he turns back.

This line reiterates the message of the first line: a man who acts as the father of his family must think not only of himself but of those in his care. It would be foolish to push forward into danger, and if he turns back he will be joyfully welcomed by his kin.

In the fourth line, SIX signifies:

Going forward leads to obstacles.
Remaining still he allies himself
With those who are on their way.

This is a situation in which a man cannot overcome obstacles by himself; he must wait until others join him in an alliance.

In the fifth line, NINE signifies:

He struggles against all obstacles
But friends are coming to help him.

The man is called upon to give assistance in an emergency, and even though the dangers he faces may be too much for him, he bravely opposes himself to them. His example attracts others whom he effectively organises so that the obstacles may be finally overcome.

In the sixth line, SIX signifies:

Going forward leads to obstacles
Remaining still brings great good fortune.
Now is the time to see the great man.

This is the sage who may move spiritually as he pleases. But his own practical nature constantly draws him back to the world, where his example and his teaching can bring good fortune both to himself and to others.

The Masters of the Four Directions: north, west, south and east. From a thirteenth century talisman

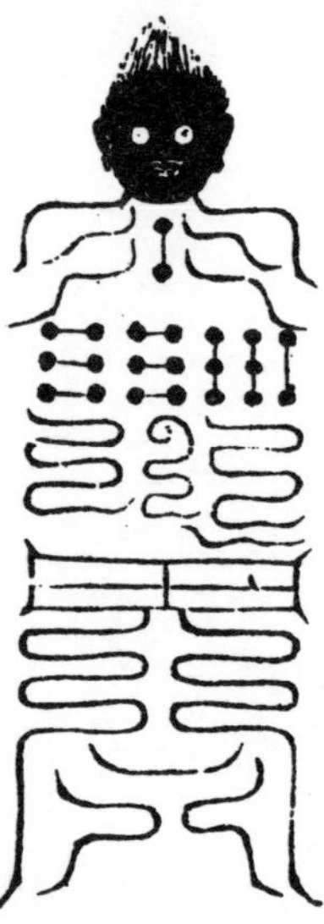

Deliverance

The trigrams:

above: Chen thunder and awakening
below: K'an water, dangerous pit

This hexagram represents deliverance from the dangers of the previous hexagram. The obstacles have been removed, troubles are resolved. However, deliverance is only beginning, and the lines of the hexagram represent its progressive stages.

The Judgment

There is advantage to the south and west. Those who have no good reason to go forward will gain good fortune by turning back. Those who have a destination in view should hasten forward to be sure of success.

Commentary

Hsieh represents deliverance from danger by activity. South and west are favourable, for those who go in this direction, that of retreat, will be loved by all; and turning back brings good fortune and makes it possible to follow the middle way. But those with a good reason to go forward should hurry on their way. When heaven and earth are released from the clutch of winter as thunder and rain, the buds of fruit trees and every sort of plant burst open. Great indeed are events in the time of Hsieh!

The Image

Thunder and rain begin, the image of deliverance. The superior man forgives mistakes and pardons crimes.

The Lines

In the bottom line, SIX signifies:
No error!

The obstacles have been removed, the barriers lifted. There is nothing to be said at this moment, nothing to be done except to rest and be thankful.

In the second line, NINE signifies:
Taking the yellow arrow,
He kills three foxes in the field.
Righteous persistence brings success.

Commentators disagree upon the precise significance of this text. The foxes are sly and devious animals; the arrow is yellow, the colour of moderation and honour. Does the hunter kill three foxes with a single arrow – as one might say, 'three birds with one stone' – or does he receive the arrow as recognition for his qualities?

In the third line, SIX signifies:
Carrying his baggage on his back
Yet riding in a carriage
He tempts robbers to attack him.
Persistence in this course
Brings nothing but shame.

This text refers to a man who has risen from poverty, in which he was compelled to carry his belongings on his back, to a newfound wealth to which he is not yet used. As Confucius says: 'A man who is insolent toward those above him, and unyielding to those below him, tempts robbers to plot an attack upon him . . . Rich ornaments worn by a virgin are an enticement to others to despoil her.'

In the fourth line, NINE signifies:
Release yourself with your toe.
Then friends will come
In whom you can put your trust.

Here deliverance is difficult and fumbled: it is as if a man were struggling to release himself from bonds by attempting to untie them with his toes rather than his fingers. He has encumbered himself with inferior people, and must break with them before he can join with friends who truly share his beliefs.

In the fifth line, SIX signifies:
The superior man can deliver himself
And enjoys good fortune.
Proving his worthiness to inferior men.

The inferior men are difficult to rid oneself of; the superior man must first break with them in his mind, and only then will they give up their attempts to hold him back, as they perceive that he is in earnest.

In the sixth line, SIX signifies:
The prince draws his bow
And slays the falcon on the high wall.
Everything is favourable.

Still hindered from deliverance by the machinations of an inferior who is, however, in a position of importance, the superior man must make his plans, get ready the means of his release, and then act with resolve.

'The prince draws his bow'. From a ninth century life of Buddha

40 HSIEH

解

41 SUN

損

Decrease

The trigrams:

above: Ken mountain, stillness
below: Tui a pool of water, joy

This hexagram is regarded as having been formed by a change in hexagram 11 (T'ai, Peace), the strong yang line in the third place having been replaced by the weak yin line from the top place; so that what is below has been decreased to the advantage of what is above. It is as if the foundations of a building had been weakened while the upper walls were strengthened.

The Judgment

One who effects decrease with sincerity will bring about great good fortune without blame. Righteous persistence is correct, and there is advantage in every move made toward a destination. If there is doubt about how to proceed, two small bowls are sufficient for the sacrifice.

Commentary

There is loss below, but gain above, and the way leads ever upward. The line in the text concerning the use of two small bowls means that one should use whatever comes to hand. At times it is right to decrease the strong and increase the weak. Decrease and increase, filling and emptying – there is an appointed time for each.

The Image

The lake lies at the foot of the mountain, the image of Sun. The superior man controls his anger and suppresses his desires.

The Lines

In the bottom line, NINE signifies:

When work is done, hurry away:
This is not wrong.
Consider, however, how you decrease
others.

When a man has completed his own business, it is unselfish and praiseworthy for him to hurry to the aid of others; but he must calculate carefully how much additional burden he can accept, and whether the limited responsibility he can assume is really a help to them.

In the second line, NINE signifies:

Righteous persistence brings reward.
But going forward brings misfortune.
One can bring increase to others
Without decreasing oneself.

A man who wishes to be of service to others must possess a serious self-awareness and preserve his essential dignity, for someone who sacrifices his principles at the insistence of another diminishes not only himself.

In the third line, SIX signifies:

If three set out together
One is lost by the way.
But a man going forth alone
Finds company.

A group of three is not an ideal working unit, for jealousy is bound to arise. A man who begins on his own is sure to find someone who will join with him.

In the fourth line, SIX signifies:

Decreasing his faults
He finds another hurrying to rejoice.
No blame.

If a man does not recognise his own faults he will often find that even friendly people are not disposed to join with him. But as he begins to recognise his shortcomings his friends will flock round him, and there is happiness on both sides.

In the fifth line, SIX signifies:

He is increased
By many – ten pair or more – of tortoise
shells.
Great good fortune.

Tortoise shells were used in divination, and were of considerable value. To someone destined for good fortune, it will come without fail, and all the oracles will give him favourable omens.

In the sixth line, NINE signifies:

Increasing without reducing others
He is without blame.
Righteous persistence brings good
fortune.
It is favourable to have a destination.
He hires servants
But has no family or home.

Those who rise to high position without harming others bring benefits to everyone. Perseverance and hard work bring success, and the successful man is in a position to enlist the help of others. But these others are not those who will aid him in marrying or setting up a home: his actions will be devoted to public service and will be for the good of all.

'A man going forth alone . . .' Painting of the Yüan epoch by Chao Meng-fu

Increase

The trigrams:

above: Sun wind, gentleness, penetration
below: Chen thunder and awakening

This hexagram represents increase because it is a development from hexagram 12, P'i, Stagnation: the strong yang line of the upper trigram has sunk to the bottom, and is rising through the lower trigram. This expresses the fundamental conception that to rule truly is to serve.

The Judgment

It is favourable to have a destination; now is the time to cross the great water.

Commentary

There is loss above and gain below, and the joy of the people is boundless, for when those placed above behave virtuously to those below them without pride their ways are brilliantly illuminated. It is favourable to have a destination, for the way is straight and lies in the middle, leading to unexpected good fortune. Finding a wooden bridge or a boat, you may cross the great water. Increase comes at once and constantly, every day brings unhindered progress. Heaven dispenses its blessings and earth brings forth its fruits. At the appointed time, increase is everywhere.

The Image

Wind and thunder, the image of I. The superior man, seeing what is good, imitates it; recognising his faults, he corrects them.

The Lines

In the bottom line, NINE signifies:

Now is the time for great undertakings.
Great good fortune.
No blame.

He who is favoured by fate with great ability must use it to achieve something great, and those below him will willingly assist him, provided too much is not demanded of them.

In the second line, SIX signifies:

There is someone who indeed increases him.
With many pair of tortoise shells
And will not accept refusal.
Persistence brings good fortune.
The king presents his offerings to the lord of heaven.
Good fortune.

When destiny smiles on a man, everything for which he strives will come inevitably to him. But only a virtuous man, who observes all the proper forms of behaviour, will enjoy such a fate.

In the third line, SIX signifies:

He is increased by evil means
But, acting in all sincerity
He is not to blame.
Walking confidently in the centre
Bearing his jade seal of office
He reports to his prince.

The man who walks the middle way will prosper even in the midst of adversity. The jade seal that he bears is the symbol of his faithfulness.

In the fourth line, SIX signifies:

Walking in the centre
He advises the prince
And is followed.
He is the man to be used
In moving the place of government.

When it is necessary for the government to show its strength to all, the seat of the capital may be moved; in the time of the emperor Shang it was moved five times. Great trust must be placed in the man charged with the responsbility of moving it; he should be above all a virtuous man who has the wellbeing of all the people truly at heart.

In the fifth line, NINE signifies:

Be sincere and kind
Ask no questions
And great good fortune will result.
All will recognise your confidence and virtue.

This is the position of the ruler, benevolently bestowing good things upon his people without demanding their allegiance; for his kindness and goodness will be recognised by all.

In the sixth line, NINE signifies:

He brought increase to no-one
And someone sought to strike him.
He is not constant in his heart.
Misfortune.

Those in high places who neglect their duty of bringing increase to those below them will soon find themselves alone, and perhaps even attacked by those they have abandoned.

42 I

益

(Above) 'Walking in the centre, he advises the prince . . .' A minister in his scarlet robe, from the eighth century painting 'Eight officials' by Ch'eng Hung

43 KUAI

Resolution

The trigrams:
above: Tui a pool of water, joy
below: Ch'ien Heaven, the creative

Ch'ien represents the father, and Tui the youngest daughter; the strong yang lines are rising resolutely upward through the hexagram, and cannot be restrained by the weak yin line at the top. The result will be a breakthrough, like a cloudburst, or a flooded river bursting its banks. And the outcome of such a breakthrough will be a *resolution* of the state of tension that produced it. Kuai is associated with the third month of the year, when frequent rainstorms burst upon the land.

The Judgment
Everything should be reported in full at the king's court, even though frankness is dangerous. When reporting to one's own city, it is not proper to be armed. It is good to have a destination in view.

Commentary
Kuai is the symbol of displacing with determination, for the strong resolve the affairs of the weak; strength is combined with cheerfulness and determination with placidity. Reporting – possibly the guilt of a criminal – at the king's court is indicated by the single weak line above the five strong lines; the importance of a known destination is also indicated by the way in which the movement of these strong lines is brought to an end.

The Image
The lake has risen above the heavens, the image of Kuai. The superior man, accordingly, bestows his gifts upon those below him; he does not rest upon his virtues.

The Lines
In the bottom line, NINE signifies:
Mighty and proud in his strength
He advances his feet.
But he is unequal to the task
And suffers humiliation.

In the Chinese, the text employs much the same words as in the text for the bottom line of hexagram 34, Ta Chuang: there is a reference to advancing with the toes, representing an attempt to go forward by sheer brute strength, without giving proper consideration to the means or to the outcome. In such circumstances, one is likely to suffer a setback at the most damaging moment.

(Above) 'Everything should be reported in full at the King's court'

In the second line, NINE signifies:
Shouts in the night.
But he who is forearmed
Is forewarned
And has no fear.

The superior man is always on his guard and so, when there is an alarm, he does not become excited and flustered. When reason triumphs over fear, he treats difficulties as though they did not exist; as he develops his strength of character, so others submit to him without argument.

In the third line, NINE signifies:
Setting the jaw and advancing straight forward
Brings misfortune.
The superior man determines on interception.
Walking alone in the rain
He is spattered with mud
And his friends murmur against him.
No blame.

In the struggle against evil, the most obvious course is to set one's jaw firmly and nobly and plunge forward. But this is not wise. The wise man, although his resolve is firm, takes a way that will enable him to cut off the criminal, even though it may appear to be devious. Because of this he will be misjudged and thought to be inferior. But remaining true to himself and his faith, he will make no mistake.

In the fourth line, NINE signifies:
His haunches are flayed
And he walks with difficulty.
Letting himself be led like a sheep
He could put an end to his pain.
But though he hears this advice
He believes it not.

Obstinately, the man pushes forward, even though he suffers; he has an inner drive that will not let him rest. This is not the way: he should desist from his foolish course and take the advice of others. But obstinacy deafens a man to all good counsel.

In the fifth line, NINE signifies:
Like a bed of weeds,
Tenacious but shallow-rooted,
Inferior men cling to the earth.
The superior man, determined to uproot them,
Treads the middle way
And suffers no reproach.

The inferior man in a high position holds desperately to his place, and it takes dangerous determination to remove him. But one must not be deflected from the true path.

In the sixth line, SIX signifies:
There is no warning.
The end is misfortune.

At the very moment when victory appears to be in one's grasp, a moment of inattention can bring disaster.

Coming Together

The trigrams:

above: Ch'ien — Heaven, the creative
below: Sun — wind, gentleness, penetration

This hexagram is linked with the fifth month, the time of the summer solstice, when the first whisper of the darkness of the coming winter is heard, intruding upon the days of joy. This is the weak yin line, driven from the top of the preceding hexagram, furtively and unexpectedly reappearing at the bottom: it represents the female principle advancing of its own accord to meet the male. Although it signifies the pleasure of sexual intercourse, it also contains elements of danger.

The Judgment

Coming together, meaning the woman is in power. A marriage in such circumstances would be unfavourable.

Commentary

The yielding confronts the firm. A marriage with such a woman would not last long. Nevertheless, it is from such an intercourse that heaven and earth give birth to all things, and when strength is properly controlled and correctly used, everything in the world goes well. And great indeed is the importance of what is done at the right time indicated by Kou.

The Image

The wind is below the heavens, the image of Kou. Accordingly, the prince gives out his orders, proclaiming them to the four quarters of the kingdom.

The Lines

In the bottom line, SIX signifies:

The wheel is checked with a brake of bronze;
Righteous persistence brings good fortune.
It is not fortunate to have a destination.
A lean pig still struggles.

A bad influence must be constantly checked, and its ill effects will be avoided. But if the restraints are relaxed, as if allowing a chariot to move forward again toward its destination, only misfortune can result. A pig should be fat, and so it must not be allowed to run about, however hard it struggles.

In the second line, NINE signifies:

The fish is in the bag.
No error.
But it is not for the guests.

There is a difference of opinion about the interpretation of this text. The fish can be seen as a wily, untrustworthy influence that must be kept confined; but it can also be a desirable catch that should be shared with others. Not to share it can be unwise.

In the third line, NINE signifies:

His haunches are flayed
And he walks with difficulty.
Mindful of his danger
He makes no great mistake.

Going forward obstinately, even though one is suffering, is unwise. But the man who knows what he is doing will suffer no misfortune.

In the fourth line, NINE signifies:

There is no fish in the bag.
Misfortune.

It is necessary to make use of inferior people in furthering one's aims. The man who does not do so will lose them by his indifference, just when he most needs them.

In the fifth line, NINE signifies:

The medlar leaves shade the melon,
Hiding its beauty.
Then it drops as if from heaven.

The melon on the vine must be shaded with leaves so that it does not ripen too quickly and spoil. The superior man protects those below him, but does not let them know that they are in his control. Then power comes to him like a ripe fruit from the vine.

In the sixth line, NINE signifies:

He meets them with his horns.
Regrets, but no blame.

This is a man who holds himself aloof from encounters with others, rebuffing their advances from a noble sense of pride. He will be reproached for his aloofness, but he does not care about his contemporaries' opinions.

'Coming together, meaning the woman is in power . . .' A porcelain incense holder decorated in the eighteenth century by Ch'ien-lung

45 TS'UI

Congregation

The trigrams:
above: Tui a pool of water, joy
below: K'un Earth, the passive

This hexagram is related, both in its form and its significance, to hexagram 8, Pi, Seeking Unity. In Pi, dangerous deep water is over the earth; in Ts'ui, the water has gathered together into a pool, fulfilling the search for unity represented in Pi.

The Judgment

Congregation brings success. The king makes his way to the temple of his ancestors, and it is favourable to see the great man: progress and success. Righteous persistence brings its reward. Important sacrifices are made, bringing good fortune. It is favourable to have a destination in view.

Commentary

Ts'ui symbolises congregation, assembling together, union. The trigram Tui, representing willing acceptance, is joined with Tui, meaning joy. A strong yang line occupies the fifth position, the place of the ruler; hence the meaning of union. The king makes his way to the ancestral temple to make his offerings to the spirits of his forbears and so secure the prosperity of his people. Congregation is implied in the meeting with a great man, and persistence is necessary for the purpose of putting matters to right. Sacrifices must be made in accordance with the rules of heaven; and by observing the way in which all things congregate together, we learn to understand the inner nature of all things in earth and in heaven.

The Image

Above the earth, a pool of water gathering: the image of Ts'ui. The superior man, accordingly, makes ready his weapons, forearmed against the unlooked-for.

The Lines

In the bottom line, SIX signifies:
Sincerity, but without pertinacity,
Brings sometimes disorder,
At times union.
He cried out
And a grasping hand made him laugh again.
No regrets; go forward without blame.

People congregate, seeking a leader; but there are so many of them that they cannot make a common decision, each being influenced by the opinions of the others. But if they recognise their dilemma, their cry for help will be heard, and reassurance from their prospective leader is sufficient to bring unity.

In the second line, SIX signifies:
Let yourself be drawn forward
Assuring good fortune and no blame.
If you are sincere
Even a small sacrifice is acceptable.

There are subliminal forces that bring men together, and by accepting and yielding to these forces, we gain fortune and avoid all blame. Those who congregate in this way understand one another, without any necessity for explanations or formalities; just as the supreme being is satisfied with the smallest offering from a man whose heart is true.

In the third line, SIX signifies:
The congregation is sad,
For no destination seems favourable.
Yet going forward brings no blame,
Only a little regret.

Sometimes a man discovers that the group with whom he had hoped to join is without any sense of direction. It is better for him then, even though he may suffer some pain, to advance in his own way, as long as he is convinced that it is right.

In the fourth line, NINE signifies:
Great good fortune.
No blame.

This is the fourth line, the place of the minister. It represents a man who gathers people around him in the service of his prince. He is striving, not for himself but for the good of the people, and so his work is crowned with success.

In the fifth line, NINE signifies:
In his high position he gathers people together.
No blame.
If some have no confidence in him
Let him persevere in virtue
And dispose of all regrets.

There may be those who gather about a man solely because of his influential position, and not from any innate confidence in him. His only course is to gain their confidence by his example of unswerving devotion to duty.

In the sixth line, SIX signifies:
Sighing and weeping,
But no blame.

When the honourable intentions of a man are misunderstood, he will be sad that he has not brought others together. But the fault is not his, and he is not to be blamed.

46 SHENG

升

Sheng represents a new shoot pushing upward with effort, as the bamboo bursts out of the soil in this painting by Li K'an

Moving upward

The trigrams:

above: K'un Earth, the passive
below: Sun wind, gentleness, penetration

The lower trigram, Sun, also symbolises wood. This hexagram represents (rather like hexagram 3, Chun) the action of a shoot in the earth pushing upward with effort.

The Judgment

Moving upward with effort against restraint brings success. Seek out the great man and have no fears. There is advantage to the south.

Commentary

The weak line moves upward at the proper time. In this hexagram, gentleness and willing acceptance are joined together. The strong line in the central position of the lower trigram wins response from the upper trigram, indicating great progress and success. Unexpected good fortune will result from the desire to see the great man and the concomitant freedom from fear or anxiety that will result. Southward lies the way to fortune, and all desires will eventually be fulfilled.

The Image

In the bottom line, SIX signifies:

Move upward
Welcomed by those above.
Great good fortune.

This hexagram represents the unimpeded rise from obscurity and inferior origins to a position of power, and this line is the beginning of such a rise. Good fortune comes from the acceptance and confidence of those in higher positions.

In the second line, NINE signifies:

Sincere,
Though he made only a small sacrifice
He suffers no blame.

A man of strong character, secure in his convictions, will not be criticised even if he is out of tune with his surroundings and impatient with formalities.

In the third line, NINE signifies:

He moves upward
Into an unoccupied city.

The obstacles are removed: the man of ambition ascends unimpeded, like a liberator entering a city that has been abandoned by the enemy. But the text adds no promise of good fortune: perhaps the unoccupied city is only a trap to lead him into disaster.

In the fourth line, SIX signifies:

The king makes offerings on Mount Ch'i:
Good fortune and no blame.

This text refers to the time when the Chou dynasty was coming into power in China; it was prince Chou, the son of king Wen, who provided the texts for the individual lines. Wen made sacrifices at the shrine on Mount Ch'i, in his homeland district in western China, and honoured his assistants by including them in the ceremony.

In the fifth line, SIX signifies:

Righteous persistence brings good fortune
But one moves upward step by step.

As a man moves ever higher, it is essential that he should not be carried away by his continuing success. He must go steadily onward, step by step, almost hesitantly, patiently making his way without haste, overlooking nothing.

In the sixth line, SIX signifies:

Moving upward in darkness.
Unremitting persistence is favourable.

Blind ambition can lead one onward not to success but to failure. Now it is more important than ever to know exactly what one means to do and where one means to go: the outcome may still be material loss, but some advantage will be gained.

47 K'UN

Exhaustion

The trigrams:

above: Tui a pool of water, joy
below: K'an water, dangerous pit

This hexagram represents a pool which has drained away into the deep pit; the water of the pool is exhausted. Within the joyousness of Tui there is an abyss, an emptiness.

The Judgment

Though there is exhaustion and adversity, righteous persistence will lead to eventual success. There is good fortune for the truly great man, and no blame. Even though he has something to say, however, his words will not be heeded.

Commentary

Joy and danger are joined together: adversity comes from something that lies hidden. He who succeeds in spite of the difficulties that face him is certainly one of the truly great; the strong line in the fifth place indicates that righteous persistence will bring good fortune to such a man. But since his words will not be heeded, it is most sensible of him not to speak at all.

The Image

The water of the pool has drained away; the image of K'un. The superior man will risk even his life to achieve the result that he wishes.

The Lines

In the bottom line, SIX signifies:

Exhausted by the bare branches that
entangle him
He strays into a gloomy valley
And for three years meets no-one.

A man who is overwhelmed by adversity may lose all initiative, caring nothing for his material condition and fixing his attention soley upon his problems rather than upon their solution. Until he can begin to think constructively about his situation, there will be no way out for him.

In the second line, NINE signifies:

Exhausted, even with a meal before him.
A minister in his scarlet sash arrives;
Now is the moment to make sacrifice.
Going forward brings misfortune
But no blame.

Sitting at the table, apparently well-fed and content, one is still exhausted and oppressed by care from which there seems to be no escape. But the minister is a messenger from the prince, who is seeking able men; it is an appropriate moment to make an offering, and pray for the removal of difficulties. Nevertheless, the time is not yet ripe for setting out; all must first be prepared.

In the third line, SIX signifies:

Exhausted by the rocks that face him
He finds nothing to lean on but thistles
and briars.
Returning to his house
He finds his wife has gone.
Misfortune

This represents a man who is too easily discouraged by adversity. Although it is possible that the rocks may be climbed, or even passed by, he exhausts himself almost at the sight of them, and finds nothing reliable on which he can depend. Turning back from the obstruction to seek rest in his home, he finds that even there he can depend on nothing.

In the fourth line, NINE signifies:

He advances very slowly
Delayed by the golden carriage in front.
There are regrets, but not for long.

Here is a man who is wealthy and successful in all material things; but he has only recently come into wealth and the ways of the rich prove an obstruction to his desire to press forward spiritually. However, the underlying strength of his nature overcomes the drawbacks, and he reaches his goal.

In the fifth line, NINE signifies:

His nose and feet are cut off;
Oppression at the hands of the scarlet-
sashed minister.
Slowly, however, joy comes to him.
Now is the time for sacrifice.

The man is obstructed both above and below, and receives no assistance from those whose duty it should be to render aid to the people. Gradually, however, matters will take a turn for the better; in the meantime, offerings and prayer should be made.

In the sixth line, SIX signifies.

Exhausted by the clinging creepers,
Tottering on the edge of a cliff,
He tells himself
'If I move I shall regret it.'
But repenting former mistakes
He can go forward to good fortune.

The difficulties are slight, the clinging creepers should be easily broken; but the man is still without resolution, racked with fear that whatever he does may prove to be wrong. If only he can make up his mind, come to a decision on the basis of recognising his errors, then all will be well.

The Well

The trigrams:

above: K'an water, dangerous pit
below: Sun wind, gentleness, penetration

The trigram Sun is also associated with wood, and this hexagram, with water above and wood below, represents the well – perhaps lined with wooden boards – in which the water is lifted up in clay or wooden pitchers attached to wooden poles.

The Judgment

In Ching, we are reminded that though the place of a town may be moved, the places of its wells cannot be changed. A well neither increases nor decreases; people come and go and draw water to their satisfaction. But sometimes, just when one is almost down to the water, the rope is not quite long enough, or the pitcher breaks – misfortune.

Commentary

It is the combination of wood with water, the wood raising the water up, that gives the symbolism of the well. It is the strong yang line in the centre of the upper trigram that implies the unmoving nature of the well and its unchanging contents. The shortness of the rope indicates that we may fail to achieve what appears to be within our grasp; the breaking of the pitcher warns of certain misfortune.

The Image

Water above wood, the image of Ching. The superior man encourages people as they work, advising them how they may best help one another.

The Lines

In the bottom line, SIX signifies:

When the well is muddy
None drink from it;
When the well is old
No creatures come to it.

If a man has no spiritual qualities, he is like someone sunk in mud, and has no significance for others. In the end, he will be alone.

In the second line, NINE signifies:

Fish dart in the well water
The pitcher is broken and leaks.

The water in the well is clear, but it is not used; there are fish there to be caught, but the pitcher cannot be used for drawing water out. This represents a man who possesses good qualities that he makes no use of; he associates with inferiors, and gradually deteriorates until he can no longer accomplish anything.

In the third line, NINE signifies:

The well is cleansed, but still,
To my heart's sorrow,
No-one comes to drink from it.
Yet the water could be drawn.
If the king were wise
Many could share his good fortune.

This indicates that a capable man is at hand, but that his abilities are not recognised and no use is made of him. If only someone in high position could appreciate his talents he could do much to help the people.

In the fourth line, SIX signifies:

The well is being lined.
No error.

The well is being repaired, and it cannot be used until the work is completed. Sometimes one must devote one's energies to one's own spiritual improvement, and at this time it is impossible to help others.

In the fifth line, NINE signifies:

The well water is cool
From an icy spring
And all may drink.

A virtuous man in a position of authority is an example to everyone; he offers the water of life to all who come to him.

In the sixth line, SIX signifies:

The well is uncovered
All may draw without hindrance.
Have confidence. Great good fortune.

The really great man is like a dependable well, never running dry, forbidden to none, supplying all who come to him with spiritual nourishment; and the more people take from him, the greater his spiritual wealth becomes.

A print derived from a T'ang engraved stone of the tenth century, depicting a peasant raising water in wooden buckets

49 KO

Throwing Off

The trigrams:

above: Tui a pool of water, joy
below: Li fire, brightness, beauty

In its original sense, Ko means an animal's pelt that moults every year, or a skin that is sloughed. By extension, it can be taken to mean a great political change, a throwing off of government, or revolution; retaining at the same time the original sense of 'revolution', a turn in the wheel of time or of fate. The two trigrams making up the hexagram are the same as in K'uei (hexagram 38, Opposites), but now they are reversed, the younger daughter being above and the elder below, so that the opposites are in direct conflict like water over fire.

The Judgment

When there is revolution, none will believe in it before the day of its completion, but then there is complete success. Righteous persistence brings reward, regrets vanish.

Commentary

Water and fire extinguish each other, like two women who share the same household but whose wills are in constant conflict. The revolution must come first, before the faith of the people in it will be established. An enlightened attitude, both to the change itself and to the means by which it is brought about, will bring joy in success, making it possible to put everything to rights. It is the power of the forces of heaven and earth to bring about the renewal that is revealed in the progress of the four seasons. Tang and Wu (Ch'eng T'ang, 'the completer', the first of the Shang emperors, and Wu Wang, the son of king Wen) revolted in accordance with the will of heaven, and the people answered their call. Great indeed are the events of the time of throwing off.

The Image

Fire below water, the image of Ko. The superior man makes observations of the calendar, and determines the days and seasons.

The Lines

In the bottom line, NINE signifies:

He is wrapped in the skin of a yellow ox.

Yellow is the colour of the middle way, and the ox is the symbol of docility. The hour for change has not yet come, and the wise man will refrain from making changes until the time is ripe.

In the second line, SIX signifies:

When the day comes
Throw off.
Go forward with good fortune.
No blame.

One should always attempt first to secure reform by moderate means, but when these are unsuccessful revolution becomes necessary. Proper preparation is essential; the time must be right; and a man with the necessary abilities, and the support of the people, is required.

In the third line, NINE signifies:

Action brings misfortune.
Persistence brings danger.
But when throwing off has been three times discussed
One may commit oneself
And be believed.

This is a warning against haste and ruthlessness in initiating change, as well as against delay in the name of righteousness. The concepts should be discussed with care, and the plans given mature consideration; only then is it wise and proper to set matters in motion.

In the fourth line, NINE signifies:

Regrets vanish.
One is accepted by the people.
Throwing off brings good fortune.

He who brings about a revolution of any kind must have the necessary authority, as well as the inner strength. Because in the end the people will only support undertakings that they know to be good.

In the fifth line, NINE signifies:

The great man makes his changes
As the tiger moults his pelt.
Even before he consults the oracle
He is believed.

The tiger, a symbol of brilliance and majesty, moults his coat every year; but the stripes, even though they may change, remain as clear and visible as ever. In the same way, when a great man leads a revolution, the reasons for the changes that he makes are apparent to all. He is so confident of his actions that he does not need to seek advice by divination.

In the sixth line, SIX signifies:

The superior man makes his changes
As the leopard moults his pelt.
The inferior man changes his face.
Beginning brings misfortune.
Righteous persistence brings good fortune.

When repression has been thrown off, or when a new direction has been established, the superior man continues to make smaller changes necessary to establish the new order. The leopard is the symbol of beauty, whose moult makes only small changes in its spotted coat. Lesser men easily adapt to the new conditions; but to attempt to continue with radical changes will bring disaster. Success lies in perseverance along the middle way.

The Cauldron

The trigrams:

above: Li — fire, brightness, beauty
below: Sun — wind, gentleness, penetration

The hexagram is the image of a cauldron: at the bottom are the legs, above them the rounded belly, then the handles like ears, and at the top the rim. The cauldron is the symbol of the nourishment it contains, and it is also the sacrificial vessel. It stands in the fire, fanned by the wind.

The Judgment
Great good fortune and success.

Commentary
The cauldron represents the peace and beauty indicated by its two component trigrams, as wood (represented by Sun) and fire combine to cook the sacrificial offering. The sages of old cooked their sacrifices in order to make them more acceptable to the supreme being, and made lavish feasts to nourish their wise and capable helpers. Ting is the symbol of flexible obedience: ears are make quick of hearing, and eyesight is sharpened. The weak yin line enters and ascends to the fifth place, where it responds to the strong yang lines below. All these things indicate great progress and success.

The Image
Fire upon wood, the image of Ting. The superior man, assuming a righteous posture, holds firmly to the decrees of heaven.

The Lines
In the bottom line, SIX signifies:

The cauldron is turned over.
To empty it of decaying meat.
Taking a concubine to bear sons
Brings no blame.

Reversing the normal order of things is acceptable when the reason for the action is good. Although a concubine is regarded as a lowly person, she should be honoured for the sons she bears. Every person, no matter how inferior his station, can gain recognition for his accomplishments if he acts in a honourable way to better himself.

In the second line, NINE signifies:

The cauldron is filled
And my friends are envious.
But they cannot harm me.
Good fortune.

'My cup runneth over' says the psalmist. The man who has obtained some solid achievement will be the envy of everyone, even his friends. But, armed with his spiritual strength, he is unassailable.

In the third line, NINE signifies:

The handles of the cauldron are broken
It cannot be moved.
The fat pheasant goes uneaten.
When sudden rains come
Regret fades away
And good fortune comes in the end.

This represents a man whose abilities go unrecognised, and who is therefore rendered ineffectual; all his good qualities are going to waste. But the unexpected rainstorm, which cools the fire and the pot standing on it, is an omen of good fortune.

In the fourth line, NINE signifies:

The legs of the cauldron are broken.
The prince's dinner is spilled
And his garments splashed.
Misfortune.

Here is a man not fit for his responsibilities. He is careless and brings misfortune not only upon himself but upon his superiors.

In the fifth line, SIX signifies:

The cauldron has yellow handles
And a golden rim.
Righteous persistence brings its reward.

The problems indicated in the last two texts have been resolved: the man in authority is unpretentious and approachable. As a result he finds competent helpers; but he must remain resolutely virtuous.

In the sixth line, NINE signifies:

The cauldron has a rim of jade
Great good fortune.
Everything is favourable.

In the preceding text, the rim of gold denotes strength and purity; jade is hard, but at the same time luminously lustrous. The sage represented in the top line gives good advice to all, finding favour in the eyes of the supreme being, and bringing good fortune to everyone without concern for his personal advantage.

A ritual cauldron in the courtyard of a Chinese temple

51 CHEN

Thunderclap

The trigrams:

above: Chen thunder and awakening
below: Chen thunder and awakening

The trigram Chen, repeated here, represents the eldest son, one who is likely to take over the leadership with energy and strength. Twice a strong yang line develops below two yin lines, its energy pushing it forcibly upward; like thunder, which bursts out with a terrifying clap, the movement produces surprise and terror.

The Judgment

Chen portends success. First comes the shock, evoking apprehension and fear, then the aftermath of laughter. For a hundred miles around people are terrified, but the sincere worshipper does not let his sacrifical cup and spoon drop.

Commentary

Thunder indicates success: but the initial terror is followed by happiness. The thunder itself is like what it provokes: shouts and laughter, fearful glee. Those who are a hundred miles away are startled, and those who are close at hand are terrified. Nevertheless, someone makes his appearance who can guard the ancestral temple and the shrines of the rural gods, one who is fit to preside at the sacrifical ceremonies.

The Image

Thunder repeated is the image of Chen. The superior man, in fear and trembling, develops his virtues and examines his faults.

The Lines

In the bottom line, NINE signifies:

The thunderclap comes: oh! oh!
Laughter and cheer follow.
Good fortune.

First comes the shock and the surprise, bringing fear and trembling. One finds oneself at a disadvantage. But after the ordeal there is relief: fear teaches us a lesson from which we can learn to our advantage.

In the second line, SIX signifies:

Thunder comes closer.
Danger is at hand.
He loses every one of his possessions
And flees into the nine hills.
He should not go in search of them
For after seven days he will recover them.

On this occasion the shock is so great that one is actually in danger, and suffers crippling loss. At this time resistance to fate is foolish; the only course is to retreat to some isolated spot where the danger cannot penetrate, and within a reasonable time all will be well again.

In the third line, SIX signifies:

Thunder is everywhere,
Driving one to distraction.
Acting impetuously now
Will bring no misfortune.

When one is overwhelmed by shock, it is easy to lose one's presence of mind. But there are times when it is wise to act upon the spur of the moment: this is one of them and, even though the act of impetuousity may bring little advantage, it will certainly do no harm.

In the fourth line, NINE signifies:

After the thunderclap
The ways are deep in mud.

This is the situation in which shock has produced dazed confusion, so that one seems to move as if deep in the mire. There is little to do but wait for conditions to improve.

In the fifth line, SIX signifies:

Thunder rolls about the heavens,
Danger is at hand.
With care, nothing is lost
But there are matters for attention.

Successive shocks seem to come from all sides. Nevertheless, by maintaining a position at the centre of the disturbance, one avoids loss and is even able to accomplish something.

In the sixth line, SIX signifies:

Thunder brings chaos
People gaze around in terror.
Taking action brings misfortune,
For though we are not ourselves touched
Our neighbours are harmed.
No blame
Although our nearest speak against us.

When the shock is one suffered by a community, it is enough to keep one's head and be unaffected by the general fear: to attempt any action at this time would be foolish. Those around one, who suffer misfortune as much through their own panic as through the direct effects of the incident, will be quick to accuse and reproach, but the man who keeps his head clear in such a situation will be able to rise above all calumny.

Inaction

The trigrams:

above: Ken mountain, stillness
below: Ken mountain, stillness

In this hexagram the male principle, represented by the yang lines, is striving upward, and the female principle, represented by the yin lines, moves downward. The inaction results from the fact that these movements have come to a conclusion in each trigram.

The Judgment

Keeping the back unmoving so that one no longer feels one's body; walking out into the courtyard without noticing the people there – there is no blame.

This alludes to the practice of Taoist meditation. In what has come to be known as the 'spiritual alchemy' of Tao, the spine is thought of as a sort of still connecting three 'crucibles': one at the base of the spine, one at the level of the solar plexus behind the stomach, and the third in the head. By meditation and breathing, the sexual energy of the pelvic region is gradually distilled, ever upward, until the initiate is filled with nothing but spiritual energy and is in a state of oneness with the energies of the universe, and finally achieves immortality.

Commentary

Ken signifies resting, desisting, coming to a stop. When it is the time for inaction, that is the time to stop; when the time comes for action, then act! By action and inaction, each at its appointed time, man makes glorious progress. The inaction represented by Ken means inaction in its proper place and time. The upper and the lower trigrams exactly correspond to each other, but do not interact; hence the wording of the Judgment.

The Image

The mountains stand together, the image of Ken. The superior man, accordingly, does not move in his thoughts beyond the position in which he finds himself.

The Lines

In the bottom line, SIX signifies:

His toes are still.
No blame
Righteous persistence is advantageous.

As in the texts for hexagram 31, Hsien, and hexagram 34, Ta Chuang, the toes represent the simplest sort of movement: by keeping the toes still one stops even before one has begun to move. A man who knows the importance of inaction at the beginning will eventually find the right way, but perseverance is essential to keep him from drifting without purpose.

In the second line, SIX signifies:

His calves are still.
He cannot aid the one he follows
And is disquieted.

The feet and legs have begun a movement, as in the instinct to follow someone more powerful than oneself. But the movement is suddenly halted: he who is moving may fall, like one who discovers almost too late that the course he is pursuing is wrong, the man he is following is evilly disposed.

In the third line, NINE signifies:

His loins are still,
His spine is stiff.
Danger.
The heart is suffocated.

He who endeavours to stifle sexual desire when his mind is not prepared for it will suffer painful results. But he who understands the true purpose of Taoist meditation and practices it correctly will feel inspiration in his heart.

In the fourth line, SIX signifies:

His trunk is still.
No blame.

Inaction at this time is appropriate: the initiate is well on the way to spiritual enlightenment, even though he is not yet free from all dangers of doubt that he is right in his policy of inaction.

In the fifth line, SIX signifies:

His jaws are still.
His speech being ordered,
He has no cause for regret.

To know when to speak and when not to speak is the way to true wisdom.

In the sixth line, NINE signifies:

He is noble in his inaction.
Good fortune.

This is the goal of inaction: spiritual nobility, which brings nothing but good fortune in its train.

52 KEN

(Below) 'He is noble in his inaction. Good fortune.' From a painting attributed to the thirteenth century artist Ma Yuan

53 CHIEN

漸

Gradual progress

The trigrams:

above: Sun wind, gentleness
below: Ken mountain, stillness

In this hexagram Sun also represents wood, as a tree on a mountain, caressed by the wind, grows slowly according to the laws of nature.

The Judgment

The maiden is given in marriage, bringing good fortune. Righteous perseverance is advantageous.

Commentary

The gradual progress symbolised by Chien is like the marriage of a young woman; there is good fortune for herself and for the man she marries, and in the dowry that she brings with her. The lines move upward, each in its correct place, to the strong yang line in the fifth position, the position of the ruler. Gradually progressing in righteousness, a man becomes fit to rule his land. The unmoving quality of the mountain, conjoined with the gentleness of the wind, gives rise to inexhaustible activity.

The Image

Upon the mountain stands a tree, the symbol of gradual progress. The superior man, accordingly, abides in dignity and virtue, inclining the people to good behaviour.

The Lines

In the bottom line, SIX signifies:

The wild geese gradually approach the shore.
The younger son is in danger,
And spoken against.
But there is no blame.

The wild goose, in Chinese mythology, flies toward the sun, which represents the male principle, like a young maiden who seeks a husband; it is also a symbol of marital fidelity, for it is said that it never takes a second mate. As they approach the shore, the geese are leaving the danger of the open water for the safety of land: a young man who has set out on his way through life feels his danger greatly, and is sensitive to any criticism. But the trouble which he may suffer is through no fault of his own. (More than two thousand years after this text was written, the 'wild geese', the sons of the outlawed Irish nobility, fled from their lands to settle in Portugal.)

'Upon the mountain stands a tree, the symbol of gradual progress.' Painting by the thirteenth century artist Kao Che-bo

In the second line, SIX signifies:

The wild geese gradually approach the cliff.
They eat and drink in peace and joy.
Good fortune.

The high cliff is a place of safety where the geese can rejoice that the danger is past. In terms of the marriage referred to in the Judgment and Commentary, this line represents material success.

In the third line, NINE signifies:

The wild geese gradually approach the dry plains.
The husband goes forth
And does not return.
The wife is with child
But does not give birth.
Misfortune.
Now is the time to drive away robbers.

The dry plains are no safe place for geese; there is no food and no hiding place. The marriage represented is unsuccessful and barren; the husband risks his own life and endangers his family. But this is unnecessary: if he can avoid provoking conflict, and remain to protect his home, misfortune will be avoided.

In the fourth line, SIX signifies:

The wild geese gradually approach the trees.
Perhaps they will find a branch to perch.
No blame.

Trees, also, are unsuitable places for geese, but they may find a safe branch on which to take refuge. In marriage, one of the partners may bring stability by kind and thoughtful acts.

In the fifth line, NINE signifies:

The wild geese gradually approach the high ground.
For three years the wife is without child
But in the end all will be well.
Good fortune.

In a high position a man can very easily become isolated, perhaps from his family, perhaps from his colleagues. His relationships are sterile, and nothing is accomplished. But as progress continues misunderstandings will be cleared away, and there will be a happy reconciliation.

In the sixth line, NINE signifies:

The wild geese gradually approach the summits.
Their feathers are used in sacred rites.
Good fortune.

There is nowhere further to advance: the geese fly ever upward to heaven, as the superior man rises far beyond the reach of ordinary mortals. But still his blessings fall like the feathers of the geese, which are gathered and used in the temple rituals.

The Marriageable Maiden

The trigrams:

above: Chen thunder and awakening
below: Tui a pool of water, joy

Chen represents the eldest son and Tui the youngest daughter; the hexagram represents the older man leading a young girl through the door of his house. But the girl is not his first wife; she is his second wife or perhaps the first of his concubines. For this reason Kuei Mei is not a very fortunate omen, even though it should not be taken as referring in every case to marriage.

The Judgment

Kuei Mei is the marriageable maiden. Going forward brings misfortune, and no destination is at present favourable.

Commentary

This hexagram symbolishes the proper relationship between heaven and earth; for if heaven and earth had no intercourse, nothing would come into existence and flourish. The marriage of the younger sister is both her end and her beginning. Joy and movement together (represented by the two trigrams) – this is the image of a maiden marrying. But the inappropriate positions of the third and fifth lines indicate that going forward will bring misfortune, for the weak yin lines are mounted upon the strong yang lines.

The Image

Thunder over the water, the image of Kuei Mei. The superior man, accordingly, understands the mischief that may be made at the beginning in order to reach a lasting conclusion.

The Lines

In the bottom line, NINE signifies:

The maiden marries as a concubine.
The lame man can still walk.
Going forward brings good fortune.

The girl who enters a family in the position of first concubine is in much the same position as a man who is appointed adviser to a high minister; he has no power of his own, but although this hampers his activities he is still able to advance both himself and the matters for which he is responsible.

In the second line, NINE signifies:

The one-eyed man can still see.
The hermit can still advance himself
By righteous perseverance.

A man who neglects the affections of his concubine is like a man with one eye: he is concerned only with his own interests. But even the solitary person, man or woman, is not without virtue.

In the third line, SIX signifies:

The maiden was but a slave
And rose to become a concubine.

Desperate to improve one's position, one can take the first opportunity that offers itself. But it is likely to be only a small advance, one still implying subservience.

In the fourth line, NINE signifies:

The maiden remains unwed
Beyond the proper day.
But a late marriage comes in time.

A girl may delay her marriage, in expectation of finding the right husband, until it seems too late. But her intentions are correct, and in the end all will be well.

In the fifth line, SIX signifies:

The emperor I gave his daughter in marriage.
Her garments were not as fine
As those of her bridesmaid.
The moon is near full
And brings good fortune.

The emperor I is T'ang the Completer. He decreed that his daughters, though of highest rank, should be subordinate to their husbands (see the fifth line of hexagram 11, T'ai). The compliant modesty of the princess is shown in the simplicity of her clothes compared with that of her younger sister, the bridesmaid. She is like the moon which, shortly before it is full, shines brightly but does not yet oppose its face directly to the sun.

In the sixth line, SIX signifies:

The woman holds the basket
But there is nothing in it.
The man sacrifices the sheep
But no blood flows.
Having no destination is favourable.

The empty basket, and the sacrificed sheep that does not bleed, signify ritual form without sincerity. In such circumstances, there is no advantage to be gained from proceeding further.

A copy of a fourth century painting on a silk scroll by Ku K'ai-chih

54
KUEI MEI

55 FENG

Abundance

The trigrams:

above: Chen thunder and awakening
below: Li fire, brightness

Chen, symbolising movement, is above Li, symbolising clarity: this combination produces abundance. However, here the height of development has been reached, suggesting that such a situation will not endure indefinitely.

The Judgment

Abundance means great success: the greatness of the king is an inspiration. Do not be downhearted, for the bright sun is now at its zenith.

Commentary

Brilliance conjoined with movement signifies abundance. The king has still greater possibilities before him: he inspires his people and they respect him, he shines like a sun before the whole world. But the sun at its zenith begins to decline; the moon that has waxed begins to wane. So all that is in heaven and earth grows and diminishes according to the season; and how much truer indeed is this of men, as well as of the gods.

The Image

Thunder and lightning come together, the image of Feng. The superior man, accordingly, hears law suits, judges and inflicts the necessary penalties.

The Lines

In the bottom line, NINE signifies:

Meeting his equal
Accepting his hospitality for ten days
There is no error.
Going forward earns respect.

Those who represent the attributes of brilliance and movement are well matched; even if they spend a complete cycle of time together, the total period of affluence, the time is well spent. Nevertheless, accepting the hospitality of equals is only a temporary respite, and very soon the time comes when it is essential to one's intellectual wellbeing to go forward again.

In the second line, SIX signifies:

The shadows close in,
The polestar can be seen at noonday.
Going forward now invites mistrust and hate.
But sincere devotion
Brings good fortune.

From the depths of a mine shaft or a well, where the scattered light of the sun has been dissipated, it is possible to see the stars even at midday; the same phenomenon is visible during an eclipse. When the machinations of a powerful party obscure the brilliance of the ruler, it is a time for the wise man to give up any ideas of energetic advance, which would only earn him mistrust and envy. Nevertheless he should maintain his loyalties and his principles, for in the end all will be well.

In the third line, NINE signifies:

The shadows are thick as a great banner
And at noonday the smallest stars are visible.
Though he break his right arm
There is no blame.

All is now in eclipse: even the most insignificant persons seem like bright stars in the gloom and confusion. Even the right-hand man of the ruler is without power to undertake anything.

In the fourth line, NINE signifies:

The shadows are like a huge tent
The polestar can be seen at noonday.
He meets his prince, an equal.
Good fortune.

Even though the darkness is still unrelieved, the eclipse is beginning to pass. Meeting with a prince of equal rank indicates that the time for action is almost arrived.

In the fifth line, SIX signifies:

Light begins to appear in the sky
As after a storm.
Unexpected good fortune
And fame draw near.

The dominance of the adversary's party is waning, and the ruler is surrounded by wise and able men who propose a modest course of action.

In the sixth line, SIX signifies:

His house is full of abundance
And there is a wall about it.
Peeping out through the gate
He sees no-one
For three years – nobody.
Misfortune.

The subject of this text has gone too far: in devoting his attentions solely to material success he has cut himself off not only from his friends and associates but from his closest family.

The Wayfarer

The trigrams:

above: Li   fire, brightness
below: Ken   mountain, stillness

The mountain, Ken, is unmoving; while the fire, Li, burns upward. The two trigrams have nothing to hold them together, and so represent the separation that is the fate of the wayfarer.

The Judgment

Lu, the wayfarer, signifies success in small matters. Perseverance brings good fortune to the travelling man.

Commentary

The weak yin line in the centre of the upper trigram is freely subservient to the yang lines on either side of it. The obstinacy represented by the mountain, conjoined to the beauty of fire, indicates success in small matters, and the good fortune that will eventually come to determined wayfarers. Great is the time and great the right course indicated by Lu.

The Image

Fire upon the mountain is the image of Lu. The superior man, accordingly, is wise and cautious in imposing penalties, and does not allow lawsuits to drag on.

The Lines

In the bottom line, SIX signifies:

The wayfarer concerns himself with trifles
And so attracts calamity.

The traveller upon the way should not demean himself, or bother with unimportant matters; he is himself humble and defenceless, and so it is even more important to preserve his spiritual dignity, and avoid the disputes he finds along the road.

In the second line, SIX signifies:

The wayfarer reaches an inn,
His valuables safe in his bosom,
And finds a young servant loyal to him.

The wayfarer is well-behaved and keeps to himself; preserving his spiritual dignity, he finds a suitable resting place. In this way, he not only retains the respect of others and his own material prosperity, but he wins the allegiance of a trustworthy follower.

In the third line, NINE signifies:

Careless,
He burns down the inn,
And loses his loyal servant.
Though firm and correct,
He is in danger.

The wayfarer is rude and ill-mannered; entirely by his own fault he loses his lodging, possibly his belongings, and the loyalty of those who follow him. Whatever his plans, it would be folly to attempt to proceed with them at this moment.

In the fourth line, NINE signifies:

The wayfarer finds a roadside shelter,
He earns his living
And acquires an axe.
But still he laments
That his heart is not glad.

The traveller modestly restricts his ambition to what he can immediately achieve. He makes a living and is, at least temporarily, established in the community where he finds himself. But he is nonetheless a stranger, and must defend himself; he has not found a home.

In the fifth line, SIX signifies:

He shoots at a pheasant
But loses his arrow.
However, in the end,
He wins praise and gains high office.

The wayfarer, who has arrived near the court of the prince, tries to shoot a pheasant as a gift for his host. But although he is unsuccessful in this, and suffers a minor loss as a result, he eventually receives great benefits.

In the sixth line, NINE signifies:

The bird burns its own nest.
As first the wayfarer laughs
And then he cries and weeps.
Careless,
He loses his cow.
Misfortune.

The bird burning its own nest is the phoenix, a symbol to the Chinese of high virtue. Yet at the same time there is a suggestion in this text that carelessness is responsible for the burnt nest. The wayfarer who sees it at first behaves irresponsibly, laughing at what he conceives to be the misfortune of another; but then he experiences his own misfortune. The Chinese commentators imply that the loss of a cow through carelessness means that no news will ever be received of something lost.

'The bird burns its own nest'. A representation in porcelain of the legendary phoenix, which to the Chinese was a symbol of high virtue

'He consults a confusion of magicians and diviners'. Two magicians in the middle of performing their esoteric rites

57 SUN

Submission

The trigrams:

above: Sun wind, gentleness
below: Sun wind, gentleness

This is one of the eight double trigrams; Sun represents the eldest daughter and gentleness, but like the wind – or like wood, with which it is also identified – it has also the property of penetration. In the natural world, the wind penetrates the clouds, bringing clarity and serenity; in human affairs, it is the penetrating clarity of intelligence that uncovers the darkness of intrigue and perversity. It took the subtle philosophy of Tao to recognise that the concomitant of such penetration was willing submission – not submission to an external fate, but the 'giving way' which is the first step to victory.

The Judgment

Submission and gentleness lead to success in many minor matters. It is advantageous to have a destination in view and to visit a great man.

Commentary

Willing submission is necessary in carrying out the will of heaven. The strong yang line is correctly in the fifth place, indicating that what is willed will be fulfilled. The weak yin lines in first and fourth place are both obedient to the yang lines above them, indicating moderate success, and the advantage of movement in any direction.

The Image

Winds follow one upon the other the image of Sun. The superior man, accordingly, makes his commands known once more, and performs his tasks according to the will of heaven.

The Lines

In the bottom line, SIX signifies:
Coming and going like the wind.
He should seek advantage
In righteous persistence like a brave soldier.

Indecisiveness is often the outcome of submissiveness: this is wrong, for only the persistence shown by someone who behaves like a bold military commander can bring advance.

In the second line, NINE signifies:
He creeps beneath the bed.
And consults a confusion of magicians and diviners.
But there is good fortune and no error.

Everything is unsure. When motives are hidden and their outcome cannot be decided, it is not blameworthy to make use of any means of determining what is to come.

In the third line, NINE signifies:
He penetrates repeatedly
And must give way.
Humiliation.

It is better to reach a decision quickly than to come eventually to an impasse as a result of constant questioning.

In the fourth line, SIX signifies:
The time for regret is past.
Three kinds of game
Are found in the hunt.

The three kinds of game are appropriate especially for sacrifices to the gods, for feasting guests, and for everyday nourishment. When one occupies an important administrative position in which experience, innate modesty and decisive action can be combined, success is assured.

In the fifth line, NINE signifies:
Righteous persistence brings good fortune.
Regrets vanish,
And everything is favourable.
There is no good beginning
But a good end.
Three days before the change
And three days after
Bring good fortune.

This text promises good fortune, but it is important to make plans for there is only a limited period during which advantage can be taken of it. The beginning may not have been propitious, but almost unexpectedly the right time will make itself apparent.

In the sixth line, NINE signifies:
He creeps beneath the bed.
He loses his living and his axe.
Persistence brings misfortune.

The subject of this text is too submissive, showing humility amounting to servility. This does him no good, for as a result he loses not only his material wealth but his very means of survival.

Joy

The trigrams:
above: Tui a pool of water, joy
below: Tui a pool of water, joy

This hexagram is another of the eight which are made up of doubled trigrams. Tui is the youngest daughter, whose gentleness brings joy through the strength of the strong yang lines in the fourth and fifth place.

The Judgment
Joy means success. Righteous perseverance brings its just reward.

Commentary
Tui signifies satisfaction in gladness. In each of the trigrams there is a strong yang line in the centre, with a weak yin line above it. This shows that seeking joy through righteous persistence is the right way to accord with the will of heaven and to reach concordance with the feelings of one's fellow men. When the people are led with gladness, they forget their burdens; as they wrestle in joy with their difficulties, they even forget that they must die. The great power of joy lies in the encouragement that it can give to all.

The Image
The waters resting one upon the other, the image of joy. The superior man, accordingly, joins with his friends in discussion and practises with them.

The Lines
In the bottom line, NINE signifies:
Contented joy.
Good fortune.

Very little need be said in explanation of the texts for the lines of this hexagram, for they are very clear in their meaning. This line signifies the quiet, undemonstrative strength that contented joy confers: wordless, self-contained and free from all envy.

In the second line, NINE signifies:
Sincere joy.
Good fortune,
No regrets.

Confident in his integrity, the sincerely joyous man will not be drawn from his path by doubtful pleasures offered him by inferior companions.

In the third line, SIX signifies:
Coming joy.
Misfortune.

There is disagreement in the interpretation of this text, but it seems probable that it means that misfortune is experienced at a time when a happy event is expected; it may be that the coming joy is only postponed by temporary setback.

In the fourth line, NINE signifies:
Calculating joys to come
He is restless.
Close to misfortune
He nevertheless is happy.

Faced with the choice of a variety of pleasures, some high and some low, a man will enjoy no inner peace. But if he is aware of the danger of indulgence, and makes his decision accordingly, he will experience true joy.

In the fifth line, NINE signifies:
Putting one's trust in crumbling things
Means danger.

One may not be aware that something is beginning to crumble away; it may be an article of faith, a political system, a business enterprise, or a relationship with another person. It is important to be very much on one's guard, so as to be able to draw back when the first signs of disintegration become apparent.

In the sixth line, SIX signifies:
Joy in seduction.

This is the weak yin line at the top of the hexagram, and it represents one who gets his pleasure, both by attracting and persuading others and by succumbing himself to all kinds of meretricious attraction. He has abandoned his spiritual advancement to give himself over to the joys of the flesh and of material things.

Joy in seduction: the man desired by three sisters, a drawing from a nineteenth century album page

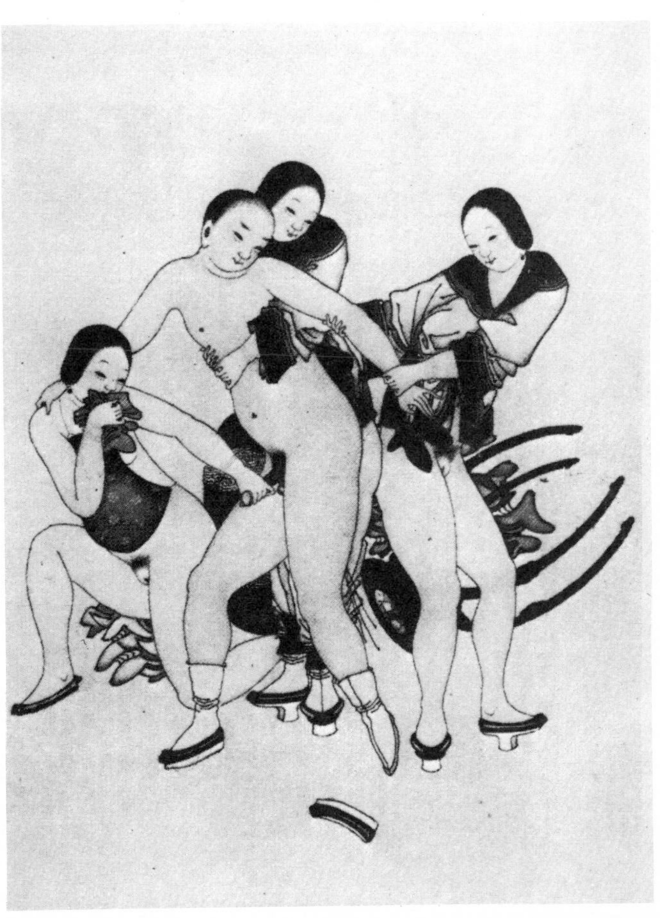

58 TUI

59 HUAN

涣

Dispersal

The trigrams:

above: Sun wind, gentleness
below: K'an water, dangerous pit

The wind blows across the water, dispersing it into spume, mists, and eventually drying it up. So a man's energy, which is dangerously dammed up within him, may be released by gentleness.

The Judgment

Huan indicates progress and success. The king approaches his ancestral temple; and it is advantageous to cross the great water, and to be righteously persistent in all.

Commentary

Successful progress is symbolised by the strong yang line in the second place, which is not exhausted there. The weak yin line in fourth place is appropriately outside the lower trigram, and the fifth line above, representing the king, responds to it. The king approaching his ancestral temple, and occupying the centre of the upper trigram, is maintaining his position without any change of mind. One of the additional attributes of Sun, the upper trigram, is wood; the advantage of crossing the great water derives from mounting upon a vessel of wood, and great success is the result.

The Image

The wind blows over the water, the image of Huan. So the kings of old built temples in which to sacrifice to the supreme being.

'So the kings of old built temples': a block-print of the early seventeenth century

The Lines

In the bottom line, SIX signifies:
He brings assistance with the strength of a horse.
Good fortune.

The wind over the water can bring clouds, and if they are not dispersed by a constant wind they will bring rainstorms. At such a time it is important to join together in vigorous action, before concealed divisions of opinion bring about misunderstanding.

In the second line, NINE signifies:
In the midst of dispersal
He hastens to the altar.
Regrets vanish.

The symbolism of the upper trigram is of a temple in which one can find shelter from the dangers of the pit below. The implication is that one should find some spiritual means of protection from the evil; and the altar represents the means that one has established to protect oneself.

In the third line, SIX signifies:
All self-interest is dispersed.
No regrets

Only by a great renunciation can a man obtain the strength to achieve great things. He must put aside all personal desires that may come between him and the welfare of others and set his sights on a goal outside himself.

In the fourth line, SIX signifies
He disperses his followers.
Great good fortune.
Dispersal leads to accumulation,
Good men standing like a mound.
Something that ordinary people
Would not have thought of.

The followers who are dispersed are those who have not proved themselves equal to their tasks. 'Cast thy bread upon the waters, for thou shalt find it after many days': the man of good intent who rids himself of incompetent companions and who continues on his self-appointed path of service to the community will soon be joined by others of a like mind.

In the fifth line, NINE signifies:
He issues his proclamations
As sweat flows from the body.
The king scatters his stores
Among the people
Without blame.

Just as a high fever is dispersed in perspiration, so the king may relieve his anxieties by dispersing his possessions among the needy. Great and generous ideas are necessary for success at this time.

In the sixth line, NINE signifies:
He disperses bloodiness
Keeping evil at a distance.
Departing without blame.

All the commentaries upon this text disagree upon the precise meaning of the words, but it seems clear that 'dispersing bloodiness' means the avoidance of bloodshed, removing oneself from the danger of injury.

60 CHIEH

Restraint

The trigrams:
above: K'an dangerous deep water
below: Tui a pool of water, joy

The word Chieh really means the joints of the bamboo, or the joints of the human frame, or the natural regular divisions of the year; thus it represents the voluntary limitations that may be set upon growth or expenditure in order to maintain matters in due moderation. The pool of water can only occupy a limited space; the movement of more water from above must be strictly restrained, or the pool will overflow.

The Judgment

Restraint brings success and progress. But restrictions that are severe and difficult should not be perpetuated.

Commentary

Chieh signifies success because the strong yang lines and the weak yin lines are equal in number, and there is a yang line in fifth position. Severe and difficult restrictions should not be allowed to continue because they produce exhaustion. Even in the midst of danger we experience pleasure and satisfaction in following the proper course. It is by the restraint exercised between terrestrial and celestial forces that the four seasons arrive each at its appointed time; so, when due restraint is shown in the duties of government, the state suffers no injury, and the people no hurt.

The Image

Water above the pool, the image of Chieh. The superior man, accordingly, creates his system of number and measure, and discusses the nature of virtue and proper conduct.

The Lines

In the bottom line, NINE signifies:
He restricts himself
To the outer gates and courtyard.
No blame.

The man who knows rightly how to limit his undertakings in the face of insuperable obstacles can accumulate an energy that, at the right moment, will enable him to act positively. Confucius says: 'Where disorder develops, words are the first steps. If the prince is not discreet, he loses his servant. If the servant is not discreet, he loses his life . . . . Therefore the superior man is careful to maintain silence and does not go forth.'

In the second line, NINE signifies:
He restricts himself
To the courtyard within his gate.
Misfortune.

When the time for action arrives, it is essential to act at once. As water flows into a pool, so there comes a moment when it must find an outlet.

In the third line, SIX signifies:
He places no restraint upon himself:
Lamentations
But no blame.

Those who give themselves up to indulgence may well have cause to regret it, but provided they are prepared to accept the responsibility for their actions they are not to be condemned.

In the fourth line, SIX signifies:
He restrains himself
Contentedly.
Success.

This text needs no further elucidation: its meaning is unambivalent.

In the fifth line, NINE signifies:
He restrains himself
Sweetly and voluntarily.
Good fortune.
Going forward brings approbation.

This is a very important line, for the strong yang line is in the position of the ruler. When a man in an important position applies necessary restraints to his own actions, without demanding too much from his associates, then his modesty will bring good fortune and it will be possible to advance with general approval.

In the sixth line, SIX signifies:
Troublesome restraint.
Persistence brings misfortune
But there is no regret.

Restrictions that are too severe will not be endured for long; even the ascetic's body will eventually rebel against self-torture. Nevertheless, on occasions a certain ruthlessness toward oneself is the only way to salvation.

61
CHUNG FU

'The crane calls in the shadows'. A detail from an embroidered coat, representing a crane with peaches to symbolise the longevity to be attained by suitable sexual practices

Inner Truth

The trigrams:

above: Sun — wind, gentleness, penetration
below: Tui — a pool of water, joy

The wind blows over the water, revealing its invisible movement in visible disturbance of the surface. The strong yang lines above and below, and the yielding yin lines in the centre, indicate a heart free from prejudice and open to the truth. At the same time, the strong line at the centre of each trigram indicates the strength of inner truth.

The Judgment

Inner truth and sincerity: the pig with the fish. This leads to good fortune. It is advantageous to cross the great water. Righteous persistence brings its just reward.

Commentary

The lines reveal joy and gentleness conjoined: confidence and sincerity will ensure the development of the kingdom. The combination of the pig with the fish may be identified as the dolphin, known in all ancient mythologies as a friendly guide upon a journey, and as one who can save a sailor from drowning: so good fortune attends any undertaking that involves crossing the great water. Persistence accompanied by confidence is always advantageous, for it accords with the will of heaven.

The Image

Wind over the water, the image of Chung Fu. The superior man, accordingly, gives thought to matters of law and delays the sentence of death.

The Lines

In the bottom line, NINE signifies:

Be prepared
As he who fishes or hunts the boar.
Good fortune.
Other intentions bring disquietude.

The angler, or the huntsman waiting in ambush for his prey, must be patient and unmoving, but ready for any emergency. But if he is unsure about his place of concealment, or finds himself in argument with others about tactics, the only result will be unease and anxiety.

In the second line, NINE signifies:

The crane calls in the shadows;
And the young ones answer.
I have a cup of contentment
And I will share it with you.

The parent crane does not reveal itself when it calls: it cries from its place of concealment, but its young still hear it and reply. This is like the response of all men of good intent when they hear the clear expression of truth. When we become aware of an important truth, we should communicate it to others.

In the third line, SIX signifies:

He finds his equal.
Now he strikes his drum,
Now he stops.
Now he weeps, and now he sings.

The equal may be an honest companion, or a worthy adversary. But one is unsure how to proceed: whether to announce the truth boldly to everyone, or to keep it to oneself; whether to rejoice in the revelation vouchsafed to one, or sorrow that it is not apparent to all.

In the fourth line, SIX signifies:

Like the moon near its fullness,
Or a team-horse whose companions have broken away.
No blame.

When the moon is at the full it stands in opposition to the sun, but at that very moment it begins to wane: so must one be modest and reverent in the face of enlightenment.

The horse pulling the carriage must continue on its way, even when its companions break free. Only in this way can one retain one's inner confidence.

In the fifth line, NINE signifies:

He seems drawn forward by his truth
And draws other with him.
No error.

The fifth line is the position of the ruler: only when his inner strength is sufficient can he carry others with him.

In the sixth line, NINE signifies:

Cockcrow rises to heaven.
Perseverance brings misfortune.

Every day at dawn the cock crows in its pride; but it cannot fly, and only its cry rises into the skies. Over-confidence in one's abilities and good fortune is followed by evil consequences.

The Small Persist

The trigrams:

above: Chen thunder and awakening
below: Ken mountain and stillness

This hexagram represents a most unusual situation: weak yin lines enclose it on both sides, and preponderate; but the two strong yang lines are at the centre. These yang lines exert their influence, creating conflict and exceptional conditions; but it is the yin lines which must relate to the external world. A man who attains a position of authority for which he is not really adequate must exercise unusual prudence.

The Judgment

The small persist. Success. Righteous perseverance brings its just reward. Small things may be accomplished, but the time is not right for great things. Birds fly high, singing, but lose their tune. It is better not to strive upward, but to stay below.

Commentary

This hexagram indicates success for the small; their persistence will be rewarded, and their deeds fit the times. The yin line in fifth place signifies success in small affairs, and good fortune. The yang line in fourth place has not succeeded in reaching a ruling position, indicating that it is not the moment for great matters. The symbol of a bird denotes that it is better to descend than to ascend; this is the way to good fortune.

The Image

Thunder upon the mountain, the image of Hsiao Kuo. The superior man, accordingly, shows excess in his reverence, too much grief in his bereavement, and too much economy in his husbandry.

The Lines

In the bottom line, SIX signifies:

The bird flies upward
And meets misfortune.

The young bird that flies too soon, before it is fully fledged, is courting disaster. Exceptional measures should only be taken when there is nothing else left.

In the second line, SIX signifies:

Passing by the ancestor
And meeting the ancestress:
Failing to see the prince
But encountering a minister.
No blame.

In the temple, the grandson stands on the same side as the grandfather. To pass by the tablets of the male ancestor, going toward those of the ancestress, is unusual, but it still shows proper reverence and humility. In the same way it is proper, having failed to secure a meeting with the prince, to make an appointment with one of his ministers.

In the third line, NINE signifies:

Take unusual precautions
For subordinates may come from behind
To strike you.
Misfortune.

At certain times extraordinary caution is necessary. There are many who, conscious of their righteousness, think it petty to keep on their guard against the subterfuges of their subordinates; but the wise man is vigilant at all times.

In the fourth line, NINE signifies:

No blame.
He meets him in his path
And does not slip by.
Going forward brings danger
Be on your guard.
Now is not time for action
But for constant determination.

The yang line is not in a dominant position, and although it tries to exert its force, there is no blame if the correct course is taken. Nevertheless, all opposition and obstacles in the path must be met face-on; but it is not the time for pushing forward.

In the fifth line, SIX signifies:

Dense clouds
But no rain from the western marches.
The prince shoots his arrow
Hitting the man in the cave.

The image of the bird has become that of high flying clouds. But though they are dense, no rain falls, suggesting that what is to come from the west is not misfortune. The fifth line represents the prince, but the two yin lines at the top represent a cave; a man in authority exercises the powers that have been given to him, but in doing so he exceeds his abilities, and injures another who represents no threat to him.

In the sixth line, SIX signifies:

He passes by
Not facing him.
The bird flies away,
Meaning misfortune.
Calamity and injury.

To go by, not acknowledging the existence of obstacles, is arrogant. Overshooting the target, one misses it: the bird escapes, but only to encounter a more successful hunter. Small things prosper, but pushing forward only brings down upon oneself misfortune and pain.

62

HSIAO KUO

(Right) Ancestral commemorative tablet of painted wood

63 CHI CHI Climax and After

既濟

The trigrams:
above: K'an dangerous deep water
below: Li fire, brightness

This hexagram represents an evolutionary phase of hexagram 11, T'ai, Peace. The strong yang lines have moved upward into their appropriately strong positions, displacing the yin lines into their proper weak positions. Everything is in its proper place. But although this is a very favourable hexagram, it still gives grounds for caution: for it is when equilibrium has been reached that any sudden movement may cause order to revert to disorder.

The Judgment
After the climax there is success in small matters. Righteous persistence brings its reward. Good fortune in the beginning, but disorder in the end.

Commentary
Chi Chi indicates progress in small matters. The proper position of the yang and yin lines shows that righteous persistence will be rewarded; the weak line at the centre of the lower trigram indicates good fortune in the beginning, but the way peters out, efforts come to an end, and disorder returns.

The Image
Water over the fire, the image of Chi Chi. The superior man, accordingly, gives due thought to the misfortunes to come, and takes precautions in advance.

'It is the neigbour in the west, with his small spring sacrifice . . .' From a fifteenth century block-print

The Lines
In the bottom line, NINE signifies:
Like a driver who brakes his chariot,
Or a fox with a wet tail.
No blame.
When all things are pressing forward, the wise man does not allow himself to be carried away by the general fever of enthusiasm. He may not be entirely unaffected by the disasters that overwhelm his companions, but he is like a fox who, having safely crossed the water, has got only his tail wet.

In the second line, SIX signifies:
She loses her carriage curtain.
Do not run after it
For in seven days it will be recovered.
In China it was a breach of propriety for a woman to drive in a carriage without a curtain. This hexagram represents someone who does not have the confidence of those in authority above him, although he feels that he deserves it. His first thought will be to try to draw attention to himself, to seek further promotion; this is wrong, for he should wait patiently until he is recognised for what he is.

In the third third line, NINE signifies:
The Illustrious Ancestor
The emperor Wu Ting
Attacked the country of devils.
Three years he took in subduing it.
Small men are not fit for such enterprises.
Wu Ting, one of the ablest of the Shang dynasty, led an expedition against the barbarous tribes on his northern borders about 1324BC. When peace and stability have been achieved, there is almost always some rebellious influence which must be overcome: frequently a tedious and bitter struggle ensues, and only a great man is suitable for the task.

In the fourth line, SIX signifies:
The finest clothes turn to rags.
Be careful all day long.
The wise man is not deceived by present prosperity: he knows that even the best things deteriorate and must be renewed, and so he is constantly on his guard against misfortune.

In the fifth line, NINE signifies:
The neighbour in the east sacrifices an ox:
But it is the neighbour in the west,
With his small spring sacrifice,
Who is blessed for his sincerity.
The neighbour in the west does not make ostentatious gestures; at the right moment, he makes his offering with proper sincerity, and so gains good fortune.

In the sixth line, SIX signifies:
His head is in the water.
Misfortune.
The man who has safely crossed water, and then gets his head wet, can only have done so by turning back; if he goes forward without looking back, however, he will escape misfortune.

64 WEI CHI

Before Climax

The trigrams:

above: Li fire, brightness
below: K'an dangerous deep water

This hexagram is the reverse of the previous one: the transition from disorder to order is not yet complete. Chi Chi is associated with autumn, when the year's growth is complete, but Wei Chi is associated with the burgeoning of spring.

The Judgment

Success. The little fox has almost crossed the water, but gets its tail soaked. No destination is favourable at present.

Commentary

This hexagram indicates progress and success because the weak yin line in the fifth position occupies a central position in the upper trigram between the two yang lines. The little fox has crossed the stream, but he has not yet succeeded in getting past the middle of the danger. The fox's wet tail and the fact that no destination is favourable imply that there is no way at present of advancing one's affairs. Although the yin and yang lines are not in their proper places, they nevertheless accord suitably with one another.

The Image

Fire over the water, the image of Wei Chi. The superior man, accordingly, carefully distinguishes between the nature of things, and between the various places that they occupy.

The Lines

In the bottom line, SIX signifies:

His tail is soaked:
Disgrace.

When the times are in ferment, there may be a temptation to push one's way forward in order to achieve something while there is an opportunity. But such precipitancy can lead to failure and humiliation if the time is not ripe.

In the second line, NINE signifies:

The driver brakes his chariot.
Righteous persistence brings its reward.

The time for action is not yet here. The subject of this line shows his persistence in his determination to slow his chariot by applying the brake.

In the third line, SIX signifies:

The destination is not yet reached,
And going forward brings misfortune.
Nevertheless
It is advantageous to cross the great water.

Although the time to go forward to the climax has arrived, one is not yet properly prepared. However, it is essential to preserve one's determination to advance as soon as the conditions become sufficiently favourable.

In the fourth line, NINE signifies:

Confident and trusted, he may drink in celebration.' One of the earliest examples of a human figure in Chinese sculpture

Righteous persistence brings good fortune.
Regrets vanish.
To subdue the country of the devils
Took great effort
But after three years
Vast territories were won.

As in the previous hexagram, this is a reference to the campaign of Wu Ting. Only perseverance will bring success in times of struggle.

In the fifth line, SIX signifies:

Righteous persistence brings good fortune
Regrets vanish
The superior man shines forth
In sincerity.
Success.

Victory has been won. All has gone well, perseverance has triumphed, and the successful outcome has justified the action. He who has achieved all this makes his influence felt amongst all men, and gains their confidence. But he should remember to be generous in sharing his good fortune with the followers who have contributed to his successful undertaking.

In the sixth place, NINE signifies:

Confident and trusted
He may drink in celebration.
No blame
But if he wet his head,
He loses all.

Now, at the moment of achievement before climax, is the time to celebrate success; and since the way forward may make many hard demands, there is no blame. But the man who carries his celebration to excess will lose the trust of others as quickly as he has won it.

INDEX TO THE HEXAGRAMS

Lower trigram	Upper trigram	Hexagram
☰	☰	1 CH'IEN
	☱	43 KUAI
	☲	14 TA YU
	☳	34 TA CHUANG
	☴	9 HSIAO CH'U
	☵	5 HSÜ
	☶	26 TA CH'U
	☷	11 T'AI

Lower trigram	Upper trigram	Hexagram
☲	☰	13 T'UNG JEN
	☱	49 KO
	☲	30 LI
	☳	55 FENG
	☴	37 CHIA JEN
	☵	63 CHI CHI
	☶	22 PI
	☷	36 MING I

Lower trigram	Upper trigram	Hexagram
☱	☰	10 LÜ
	☱	58 TUI
	☲	38 K'UEI
	☳	54 KUEI MEI
	☴	61 CHUNG FU
	☵	60 CHIEH
	☶	41 SUN
	☷	19 LIN

Lower trigram	Upper trigram	Hexagram
☳	☰	25 WU WANG
	☱	17 SUI
	☲	21 SHIH HO
	☳	51 CHEN
	☴	42 I
	☵	3 CHUN
	☶	27 I
	☷	24 FU

Lower trigram	Upper trigram	Hexagram
☴	☰	44 KOU
	☱	28 TA KUO
	☲	50 TING
	☳	32 HENG
	☴	57 SUN
	☵	48 CHING
	☶	18 KU
	☷	46 SHENG

Lower trigram	Upper trigram	Hexagram
☶	☰	33 TUN
	☱	31 HSIEN
	☲	56 LÜ
	☳	62 HSIAO KUO
	☴	53 CHIEN
	☵	39 CHIEN
	☶	52 KEN
	☷	15 CH'IEN

Lower trigram	Upper trigram	Hexagram
☵	☰	6 SUNG
	☱	47 K'UN
	☲	64 WEI CHI
	☳	40 HSIEH
	☴	59 HUAN
	☵	29 K'AN
	☶	4 MENG
	☷	7 SHIH

Lower trigram	Upper trigram	Hexagram
☷	☰	12 P'I
	☱	45 TS'UI
	☲	35 CHIN
	☳	16 YÜ
	☴	20 KUAN
	☵	8 PI
	☶	23 PO
	☷	2 K'UN